Oneness
a n d
Trinity
A.D. 100–300

Oneness and Trinity

A.D. 100-300

The Doctrine of God
in Ancient Christian Writings

BY DAVID K. BERNARD

Oneness and Trinity, A.D. 100-300

by David K. Bernard

©1991 David K. Bernard

Printing History: 1992, 1994, 1996, 1998, 2002

Cover Design by Tim Agnew

All Scripture quotations in this book are from the King James Version of the Bible unless otherwise identified.

Printed in United States of America

Printed by

WORD AFLAME®PRESS
8855 DUNN ROAD
HAZELWOOD, MO 63042-2299

Library of Congress Cataloging-in-Publication Data

Bernard, David K., 1956-
     Oneness and trinity, A.D. 100-300: the doctrine of God in ancient Christian writings/by David K. Bernard.
        p.   cm.
     Includes bibliographical references and index.
     ISBN 0-932581-81-1:
     1. God—History of doctrines—Early church, ca. 30-600.
     2. Trinity—controversial literature. 3. Oneness doctrine
(Pentecostalism)   I. Title.
BT98.B39   1991   90-29268
231'.044'09015—dc20   CIP

Contents

. . . .

Introduction

1

Studying Oneness and Trinity in Ancient Writings

The Oneness Pentecostal movement teaches that the biblical, apostolic, Christian doctrine of God, which it commonly calls Oneness, excludes the modem doctrine of the trinity. This statement gives rise to at least two historical questions. First, if the trinitarian dogma is not biblical, when and how did it become part of Christendom? Second, what beliefs about God do the earliest postbiblical Christian writings express—Oneness, trinitarianism, or something else?

To answer these questions, this book will analyze the oldest existing writings produced in Christendom after the completion of the New Testament. The earliest of these date from approximately A.D. 100, and we will carry our investigation into the next two centuries, to approximately A.D. 300.

In order to conduct this study, we must first define the two doctrinal systems for which we will seek evidence, identify the writings we will consider, and point out some limitations of our investigation.

Definition of Oneness

The doctrine of Oneness can be stated in two affirmations: (1) God is absolutely and indivisibly one with no distinction of persons (Deuteronomy 6:4; Galatians 3:20). (2) Jesus Christ is all the fullness of the Godhead incarnate (John 20:28; Colossians 2:9).

All the names and titles of the Deity, such as God, Jehovah, Lord, Father, Word, and Holy Spirit, refer to one and the same being. These various names and titles simply denote manifestations, roles, relationships to humanity, modes of activity, or aspects of God's self-revelation.

All these designations of the Deity apply to Jesus, and all aspects of the divine personality are manifested in Him. Jesus is God, or Jehovah, incarnate (Isaiah 9:6; 40:9; John 8:58; 20:28; II Corinthians 5:19; Colossians 2:9; I Timothy 3:16; Titus 2:13). Jesus is the Father incarnate (Isaiah 9:6; 63:16; John 10:30; 14:9-11; Revelation 21:6-7). The Holy Spirit is the Spirit that was incarnated in Jesus and is Jesus in Spirit form (John 14:16-18; Romans 8:9-11; Philippians 1:19; Colossians 1:27).

The Oneness doctrine recognizes that the Bible reveals God as the Father, in the Son, and as the Holy Spirit. The one God is the Father of all creation, Father of the only begotten Son, and Father of born-again believers. (See Deuteronomy 32:6; Malachi 2:10; Galatians 4:6; Hebrews 1:5; 12:9.)

The title of Son refers to God's incarnation. The man Christ was literally conceived by the Spirit of God and was therefore the Son of God (Matthew 1:18-20; Luke 1:35). The title of Son sometimes focuses solely on the humanity of Christ, as in "the death of his Son" (Romans 5:10). Sometimes it encompasses both His deity and humanity, as in "Hereafter shall ye see the Son of man sitting on the right hand of power, and coming in the clouds of heaven" (Matthew 26:64). It is never used apart from God's incarnation, however; it never refers to deity alone.

The terms "God the Son" and "eternal Son" are non-biblical; the Bible instead speaks of the "Son of God" and the "only begotten Son." The Son is not eternally begotten by some incomprehensible, ongoing process; rather, the Son was begotten by the miraculous work of the Holy Spirit in the womb of Mary. The Son had a beginning, namely, at the Incarnation (Luke 1:35; Galatians 4:4; Hebrews 1:5-6).

There is a real distinction between God and the Son—not a distinction of two divine persons, but a distinction between the eternal Spirit of God and the authentic human being in whom God was fully incarnate. While Jesus was both God and man at the same time, sometimes He spoke or acted from the human viewpoint and sometimes from the divine viewpoint. As Father, He sometimes spoke from His divine self-awareness; as Son, He sometimes spoke from His human self-awareness. As a man, He prayed to, related to, and submitted to God as all humans should do. At the same time God dwelt in and revealed Himself in that man with His undiminished character, nature, power, and authority.

In John 1, the Word is God's self-revelation, self-expression, or self-disclosure. Before the Incarnation, the Word was the thought, plan, reason, or mind of God. In the beginning, the Word was with God, not as a distinct person but as God Himself—pertaining to God much as a man and his word. "The Word was God Himself" (John 1:1, Amplified Bible). In the fullness of time God put flesh on the Word; He revealed Himself in flesh. In the person of Jesus Christ, "the Word was made flesh" (John 1:14). "God was manifest in the flesh" (I Timothy 3:16). The eternal Word was revealed in the begotten Son.

The title of Holy Spirit refers to God in spiritual essence and activity. It describes the fundamental character of God's nature, for holiness forms the basis of His moral attributes while spirituality forms the basis of His nonmoral attributes. The title is particularly used of works that God can do because He is a Spirit, such as anointing, regenerating, indwelling, and sanctifying humanity. (See Genesis 1:1-2; Acts 1:5-8.)

The three roles of Father, Son, and Spirit are necessary to God's plan of redemption for fallen humanity. In order to save us, God provided a sinless Man who could die in our place—the Son. In begetting the Son and in relating to humanity, God is the Father. And in working in our lives to empower and transform us, God is the Holy Spirit.

In sum, the titles of Father, Son, and Holy Spirit describe God's multiple roles and works, but they do not reflect an essential threeness in God's nature. *Father* refers to God in family relationship to humanity; *Son* refers to God in flesh; and *Spirit* refers to God in activity. For example, one man can have three significant relationships or functions—such as administrator, teacher, and counsellor—and yet be one person in every sense. God is not defined by or limited to an essential threeness.

A corollary of the Oneness doctrine is that the name of Jesus, which means Jehovah-Savior, is the supreme name by which God has revealed Himself to humanity and the redemptive name in the New Testament. (See

Matthew 1:21; Luke 24:47; Acts 4:12; 10:43; Philippians 2:9-11; Colossians 3:17.) Consequently, the apostles always baptized by invoking the name of Jesus, and the church should do the same today. (See Acts 2:38; 8:16; 10:48; 19:3-5; 22:16; Romans 6:3-4; I Corinthians 1:13; 6:11.) Since Jesus is all the fullness of God incarnate, the name (singular) of the Father, Son, and Holy Spirit as described by Matthew 28:19 is Jesus. (See Matthew 1:21; Luke 24:47; John 5:43; 14:26.)

Definition of Trinitarianism

Trinitarianism is the belief that there is "one God in three Persons"[1] or "three persons in one substance."[2] The unique names of these three persons are God the Father, God the Son (or Word), and God the Holy Ghost (or Holy Spirit). The three persons are distinctions in God's very being, not simply manifestations or distinctions of activity.[3] "There is in the Divine Being but one indivisible essence. . . . In this one Divine Being there are three Persons or individual subsistences, Father, Son, and Holy Spirit."[4]

Orthodox trinitarian doctrine holds that the three divine persons are (1) coequal in power and attributes, (2) coeternal in the past, present, and future, and (3) consubstantial—that is, in each person the same divine substance or essence is fully contained.[5] Each person has one unique characteristic when viewed in relation to the others: the Father is unbegotten, the Son is begotten or generated, and the Spirit is proceeding.[6] Trinitarians sometimes say that the uniqueness of the Father is displayed in creation, that of the Son in redemption, and that of the Spirit in sanctification, yet all three actively share in each work, with varying stress of functions.[7] Since each participates in the work of the others, there is no clear distinction on that basis.

Modern trinitarianism was first officially affirmed in part by the Council of Nicea in 325. It was more definitively and conclusively stated by the Council of Constantinople in 381. The result of these two councils was the Nicene Creed, or more properly, the Niceno-Constantinopolitan Creed. This creed and the so-called Athanasian Creed, which was composed sometime in the fifth to eighth centuries, are the two most accepted and authoritative statements of trinitarianism.

Oneness and Trinitarianism Contrasted

Oneness

1. There is one God with no distinction of persons.

2. The oneness of God is not a mystery.

3. Jesus is the incarnation of the fullness of God; in His deity He is Father, Word, and Spirit.

4. The Son of God was begotten after the flesh, not from eternity; the term refers to the Incarnation.

5. The Word is not a separate person but is God's mind, plan, thought, and self-revelation, which is God Himself.

Trinitarianism

1. There are three coequal, coeternal, consubstantial persons in one God.

2. The triune nature of God is an incomprehensible mystery.

3. Jesus is the incarnation of only one of three divine persons, the Son.

4. The Son is eternal and is eternally begotten; the term refers to Christ's identity as the second divine person.

5. The Word is the second divine person; the term is synonymous with the title of Son.

Oneness

6. Jesus is the revealed name of God in the New Testament.

7. Water baptism should be administered by invoking the name of Jesus.

8. To receive Christ is to receive the Holy Spirit and vice versa.

9. Believers will definitely see only one divine being in heaven: Jesus Christ.

Trinitarianism

6. Jesus is the human name of the Son of God.

7. Water baptism should be administered in the titles of Father, Son, and Holy Spirit.

8. Many trinitarians say one can have separate experiences with Christ and the Holy Spirit, or receive each on different occasions.

9. Believers will encounter the trinity in heaven. Many trinitarians say they will see three visible forms; many are uncertain or unclear.

Our historical investigation will focus on statements that assert or imply either a Oneness or a trinitarian position on one or more of these nine points. It is important to note that the simple mention of Father, Son, and Holy Spirit does not prove that a writer is trinitarian, for Oneness acknowledges these aspects of God's self-revelation. The question is whether the writer presents these terms as temporal manifestations or as eternal, self-conscious persons. A differentiation between God and the Son does not prove that a writer is trinitarian either; in fact, such a distinction is essential to Oneness. The question is whether the distinction relates to deity and humanity (to the Incarnation) or to a relationship between coeternal, coequal persons. Finally, while the belief in multiple divine persons excludes Oneness, it does not necessarily mean orthodox trinitarianism. Trinitarianism requires the belief in exactly three divine persons, and for a writer to be classified as orthodox rather than heretical by historic trinitarian standards, he cannot deny the coequality, coeternity, or consubstantiality of the three persons.

Survey of the Existing Writings

For the purpose of discussion, we will divide the time period of our investigation into three ages that historians generally recognize under one label or another:

1. The Post-Apostolic Age (c. A.D. 90-140)
2. The Age of the Greek Apologists (c. A.D. 130-180)
3. The Old Catholic Age (c. A.D. 170-325)

These dates are approximate and uncertain, as are all dates before 325 in this book. The dates overlap since the leaders and writers of one age were ending their ministry as those of the subsequent age were beginning theirs.

The Post-Apostolic Age encompasses the generation after the death of the last apostle, John, which occurred in the mid to late A.D. 90s. The leaders of this age actually began their ministry shortly before that date. It can be somewhat misleading to think of them as the immediate successors of the apostles, however. Peter and Paul were martyred by A.D. 70, and probably so were the other apostles except John. Their immediate successors were men such as Timothy, Titus, and Mark, sons in the gospel and junior colleagues of Peter and Paul.

The existing writings of the Post-Apostolic Age are (1) an epistle of Clement, bishop of Rome; (2) seven epistles of Ignatius, bishop of Antioch; (3) an epistle of Polycarp, bishop of Smyrna; (4) *The Shepherd* of Hermas, who is otherwise unknown; (5) fragments from Papias, bishop of

Hierapolis; (6) the so-called *Second Epistle of Clement*, which is actually a sermon by an unknown author; (7) the so-called *Epistle of Barnabas*, which was not written by Paul's companion; (8) fragments of the spurious *Preaching of Peter;* and (9) possibly the so-called *Teaching of the Twelve Apostles*, or *Didache*, which definitely was not written by the apostles.[8]

The authors of these documents are commonly called the Apostolic Fathers, or more accurately, the Post-Apostolic Fathers. They were active from about 90 to 140; some writings in this category are perhaps as late as 150. For the most part, these writings adhere closely to the phraseology and thought of the New Testament and offer little in the way of a theological system.

During roughly the second generation after the death of John, several writers composed apologies, or defenses of Christianity, addressed to non-Christians. Since they wrote in Greek they are called the Greek Apologists. They were active from about 130 to 180; their oldest existing writings date from about 150.

The writers whose works survive from that era are (1) Marcianus Aristides; (2) the anonymous author of the *Epistle to Diognetus;* (3) Flavius Justinus (Justin), by far the most prolific and influential Greek Apologist; (4) Tatian of Syria, a disciple of Justin; (5) Melito, bishop of Sardis, of whose writings only fragments remain; (6) Theopbilus, bishop of Antioch; and (7) Athenagoras, reportedly of Athens.[9] We have a few insignificant fragments from other authors; many works from this time are lost.

The Greek Apologists, most notably Justin, strove to make Christianity acceptable to their pagan contemporaries. To do so they identified Christian beliefs with

Greek philosophical ideas as much as possible, which inevitably led to doctrinal impurities. The following quotations represent the consensus of scholars on this subject:

> Rationalism and moralism are the distinctive marks of the Christianity of the Apologists. . . . In content their theology hardly differs from the idealistic philosophy of their contemporaries. . . . In passing critical judgment upon the Apologists, it must be remembered that every practical apologetic proof forced them to accommodate themselves to the language of their opponents. . . . The method, however, becomes dangerous. In the course of time, language will inevitably affect the content of its message. In this respect the Apologists set a bad example for succeeding generations.[10]

> The Greek Apologists . . . themselves being Gentile Christians and under the influence of the civilization of the age were bent on harmonizing Christian truth with Hellenistic philosophy. . . . As they conceived of Christian truth as a new improved philosophy they failed to give Christianity its full value as the religion of salvation.[11]

> Harnack and Loofs are of the opinion that the Apologists completely fell away from the right apprehension of the Christian Gospel . . . especially through their Logos doctrine. . . . It must be admitted that they represented Christianity largely in terms of philosophy, that they did not clearly discriminate between philosophy and theology, and that their rep-

resentation of the truths of revelation, and particularly of the Logos doctrine, suffered from an admixture of Greek philosophical thought.[12]

The writers of the Old Catholic Age built upon the work of the Apologists. We call this age "catholic," which literally means universal, because it saw the beginning and partial development of a formal system of theology to define universal orthodoxy against various heresies. It is "old" in relation to the Ecumenical Catholic Age (325-787), the age of the ecumenical councils beginning with the Council of Nicea in 325, in which church leaders further defined and solidified a doctrinal system.

We can classify the leading writers of the Old Catholic Age in three major schools of thought identified by geographical location.[13]

1. Asia Minor: (a) Irenaeus, who was from Asia Minor but who became bishop of Lyons in Gaul; (b) Hippolytus, who studied under Irenaeus and later led a small church in Rome in opposition to the bishop there.

2. Alexandria: (a) Clement, a local church presbyter (elder) and head of a theological school in Alexandria; (b) Origen, a local church presbyter in Alexandria who taught in Clement's school and succeeded him as head and who was excommunicated by his bishop.

3. North Africa: (a) Tertullian, a local church presbyter in Carthage who broke away from the main church to join the Montanists; (b) Cyprian, a student of Tertullian and later a bishop in North Africa.

We will briefly examine some other writers from this time, but we will particularly focus on the most significant doctrinal writers: Irenaeus, Tertullian, and Origen.

We will investigate the evidence during this time for baptism in the name of Jesus and for the prevalence of Oneness concepts among the common people. We will also seek to ascertain the beliefs of the modalists, particularly Praxeas, Noetus, and Sabellius, the leading teachers. The modalists affirmed the absolute oneness of God and the full deity of Jesus Christ while rejecting concepts of trinitarianism. We will attempt to discover how their teachings relate to modern Oneness.

Although the Arian doctrine arose toward the end of this age and became the chief rival of trinitarianism in the fourth century, we will not analyze it, for doing so would require a thorough discussion of the Council of Nicea and post-Nicene developments, which is beyond the scope of this book.

Limitations in Studying Ancient Documents

It is important to note several difficulties in using these documents to determine ancient doctrinal positions.

1. There is always the possibility and even likelihood of changes or insertions (interpolations) by copyists. The manuscripts we have are hundreds of years later than the originals, and some exist only in translations. Many ancient scribes and translators had few qualms about changing statements they did not accept or adding statements to support their own doctrine. A few even acknowledged doing so, like an editor. Thus it is unwise to rely upon an isolated statement in defining the views of a particular writer, and in some cases we may never know exactly what an original writer said or meant.

2. We must take doctrinal biases into consideration. First, many changes or insertions were undoubtedly made by copyists after trinitarianism became dominant in the fourth century, for most of the existing manuscripts date from long after that time. Second, church and state authorities in later ages often destroyed writings that they judged to be unorthodox. Third, deliberately or not, writers probably misrepresented the views of their doctrinal opponents, whose works usually have not survived, and later accounts of a controversy would be even more prone to distortion. There is much truth in the statement that history is written by the victors.

3. Existing documents may not always reflect the views of the average believer of their time. First, the selective destruction of works means that what we now have may not be representative of the total body of writings from a certain time. Second, in many cases, those who had the education, leisure, and motivation to write were not necessarily typical. Many existing documents were written by people who had no official position in the church of their day, or only a minor position, and some of these authors were actually rejected by their church. Some of them admitted that the majority of believers opposed their views.

4. False doctrines existed from the earliest times, as many New Testament examples, warnings, and predictions show. The antiquity or popularity of a document is no guarantee of its doctrinal purity. Moreover, with the exception of John and his writings, the apostles had died and the New Testament had been written by about A.D. 70, which places the earliest postbiblical writings about twenty to fifty years, or a generation, after the main thrust of apostolic ministries and writings. In the intervening time, false doctrines and false prophets became rampant, and entire churches forsook the faith. (See II Timothy 1:15; I John 4:1-3; Revelation 2-3.)

5. *The writings we will analyze are not inspired or infallible.* Therefore, it is a mistake to base doctrine upon them instead of Scripture.

Some trinitarians claim that we should appeal to these writings to help resolve disputes over Scripture. An example is the following comment regarding second-century writings:

> These writings and authors are not, like the canonical writings, absolutely authoritative for our faith, but they do serve as indispensable aids in interpreting the canonical writings, especially on disputed subjects. The reasoning here is simple: religious traditions take time to emerge. . . .
>
> It is exceedingly difficult for us to conceive of the Christian leaders of the early second century . . . as grossly misunderstanding and distorting what that doctrine was. To say the very least, the Apostles would have had to have been *extremely* poor teachers of truth and the Holy Spirit a very weak protector of truth if that were the case.
>
> If, then, what we *think* the original disciples of our Lord meant to teach differs significantly from what the generations immediately succeeding these disciples understood them to teach, chances are *we* are understanding the teaching of the original disciples *wrongly.*[14]

This argument implies that postbiblical writers were clearer and more definitive on the true doctrine of God than the biblical writers themselves. If so, it would appear that the apostles were poor communicators and the Holy Spirit a poor inspirer. It is a mistake to say that we can understand doctrinal truth better in the early postbiblical writings than in the Bible itself and therefore should use them to interpret the Bible.

In effect, such an approach could establish extra-biblical writings as authorities, and "indispensable" ones at that. If we use these writings as definitive interpreters of Scripture or appeal to them to resolve disputes over the meaning of Scripture, then in practice we elevate their authority above that of the Bible. Such an approach undermines the sole authority of Scripture, a fundamental tenet of Protestantism. The Roman Catholic Church uses a similar method, claiming the sole authority to interpret Scripture and regarding church tradition as equal in authority to Scripture. Likewise, groups such as Jehovah's Witnesses, Mormons, and Christian Scientists claim to use the Bible as their authority but actually depend on extrabiblical writings to interpret Scripture or define doctrine.

In any case, many trinitarians today are inconsistent in appealing to postbiblical writings. For example, the significant writers of the first five centuries agreed that water baptism is necessary to salvation, but most Protestants today reject this doctrine. The Nicene Creed confesses faith in "one baptism for the remission of sins," but most Protestants do not believe these words or else reinterpret them contrary to the intent of the creed's framers. Similarly, Protestant church historians typically criticize early postbiblical writers for legalism and assert that Martin Luther in the sixteenth century was the first writer after the apostle Paul to clearly state the doctrine of justification by faith alone.

With respect to the Godhead, none of the second-century writers clearly expressed trinitarian orthodoxy, and many of them denied it by such doctrines as the subordination of one divine person to another. As trinitarian scholars generally concede and as chapter 7 documents, even in the third century most champions of trinitarianism expressed their doctrine in the language of tritheism (belief in three gods) and subordinationism, which trinitarians today consider heretical.

The usual trinitarian response is that we should not judge these writers by the standards of later precision and orthodoxy. But this response implies that the Bible is not a sufficient standard for determining orthodoxy, for the Bible itself (whether interpreted by trinitarians or Oneness believers) shows that such language is inappropriate and such concepts are false. Moreover, this response concedes that the doctrine of trinitarianism developed through a lengthy historical process. Finally, it argues that the earliest postbiblical writers were the *least* accurate in presenting the scriptural doctrine of God and that theologians two and three centuries after the completion of the New Testament understood and explained the doctrine better than all those before them. This conclusion undercuts the rationale given for appealing to postbiblical authorities in the first place, namely, the argument that the closer we go back to the apostles the more clear and orthodox are the writers.

In sum, the study of these ancient documents cannot substitute for, or aid significantly in, the study of Scripture itself. We cannot appeal to them as authorities or base our doctrine upon them. We use them simply to help ascertain what beliefs were current among professing Christians in postbiblical centuries.

The
Post-Apostolic Age,
A.D. 90-140

2

Clement, Ignatius, Polycarp, and Hermans

To begin our investigation, we will analyze the four major authors in Christendom whose writings survive from the generation immediately after the death of the last apostle, John. They ministered or wrote from approximately A.D. 90 to 140. Chapter 3 will analyze anonymous and pseudonymous writings from the same time. It is probable that there were a number of other significant Christian writers during this time, but their works have not survived.

The four writers we will discuss in this chapter are Clement, bishop of Rome; Ignatius, bishop of Antioch; Polycarp, bishop of Smyrna; and Hermas, of whom nothing further is known definitely. The three bishops were pastors of the churches in their respective cities. All three churches were established in apostolic times and were quite prominent; thus it is likely that these bishops' views carried weight. The writing of Hermas was quite popular in the second century and probably reflected typical church practices and lifestyle. The author apparently held no significant position in the church, however, so it is impossible to say how representative or accepted some of his views were.

We now turn to an analysis of the writings of each man with respect to the doctrine of God. Dates of composition are given in parentheses. Although they are the consensus of scholars, they are approximate and uncertain.

Clement of Rome

Clement's *Epistle to the Corinthians*, or *I Clement* (c. 96), affirms that God is one, calling God "the Holy One" (30) and the "merciful and compassionate One" (60).[1] Clement wrote, "Thou art God alone and Jesus Christ [is] Thy Son" (59).

Clement identified Jesus Christ as God. "Our Lord Jesus Christ [is] the Sceptre of the majesty of God" (16). "Christ . . . Himself by the Holy Ghost thus addresses us [in Psalms]" (22). As Jesus, God suffered for the church: "Content with the provision which God had made for you, and carefully attending to His words, ye were inwardly filled with the doctrine, and His sufferings were before your eyes" (2). Significantly, in the third century, trinitarians such as Tertullian denounced the idea that God could suffer, ridiculing their opponents, the modalists, for teaching that the Father suffered in Christ.

Clement called God the "Father and Creator of the universe" (19); "Creator and Lord of all" (20, 33); "Creator and Father of all worlds, the Most Holy" (35); and "only Benefactor of spirits and God of all flesh . . . the Saviour of those in despair, the Creator and Guardian of every spirit" (59). In short, he identified the Father as our Creator, Savior, and Lord, which are biblical titles of Jesus. He also consistently referred to Jesus as "our Lord" (1, 20).

Clement placed emphasis on the singular name of God, as the following phrases show: "His all-holy and glorious name" (58); "the most hallowed name of His majesty" (58); "Thine almighty and all-excellent Name" (60); "our hope resting on Thy name" (59); "to the well-pleasing of His name" (64); "every soul that calleth upon His glorious and holy Name" (64). The last phrase possibly alludes to the Jesus Name baptismal formula, much like Acts 15:17, 22:16, and James 2:7, as Cyril Richardson's translation indicates: "Every soul over whom His magnificent and holy name has been invoked."[2]

Only two sentences in *I Clement* could imply a trinity. Chapter 46 asks, "Have we not (all) one God and one Christ? Is there not one Spirit of grace poured out upon us?" (46). This language appears to be an allusion to Ephesians 4:4-6, which speaks of one body, one Spirit, one hope, one Lord, one faith, one baptism, and one God and Father. The key thought in both passages is oneness, not threeness. Ephesians 4:6 shows that the titles of Lord and Spirit relate to the one God, who is the Father: "One God and Father of all, who is above all [i.e., who is Lord], and through all, and in you all [i.e., who is the Spirit in you]."

The other sentence is found in chapter 58, which exists in only one Greek manuscript, dated 1056, and which is missing from the only other Greek manuscript we have. The relevant sentence is: "For as God liveth, and as the Lord Jesus Christ and the Holy Ghost live—both the faith and hope of the elect, he who in lowliness of mind, with instant gentleness, and without repentance hath observed the ordinances and appointments given by God—the same shall obtain a place and name in the number of those who are being saved through Jesus Christ, through whom is glory to Him for ever and ever." In the original Greek, the first part of this phrase literally reads, "For as God lives and the Lord Jesus Christ lives and the Holy Spirit, not only the faith but also the hope of the elect ones. . . ."

This phrase is not explicitly trinitarian. Significantly, it does not use "Father" and "Son," the unique names of the first two divine persons according to trinitarianism. Moreover, immediately before this sentence, the passage speaks of God and of His name in the singular. The quoted sentence again speaks of God in the singular, and it discusses the salvation we have from God through Christ. It concludes by giving praise to God through Jesus Christ, using a twofold reference and not a threefold reference.

The focus of the passage is upon our salvation, as indicated by the use of "faith," "hope," "elect," and "being saved," not upon the doctrine of God. In this context the quoted phrase simply refers to the living God, to the glorified Christ through whom God has provided salvation and through whom He reveals Himself now and for eternity (Revelation 22:3-4), and to the regenerating work of God's Spirit.

Ignatius

An early but unproved tradition, which editor A. C. Coxe of *The Ante-Nicene Fathers* accepted, says that Ignatius and Polycarp were fellow disciples under the apostle John.[3] The writings of Ignatius (c. 110-15) equate Jesus with the one God so strongly that some historians have called his doctrine modalistic.

We have seven genuine letters of Ignatius, along with six spurious ones from the fourth century and three spurious ones from the twelfth century. The *Martyrdom of Ignatius* dates to the fifth century. Richardson stated that the genuine letters of Ignatius exist in an abridged Syriac version, a long version filled with fourth-century interpolations (insertions), and a medium version that is the most accurate.[4] There is much dispute among scholars regarding the original wording of the letters. The longer version frequently "corrects" statements contradictory to trinitarianism and adds statements more in harmony with trinitarianism, as shown by the closing remarks in three of the letters:

Medium version	Long version (interpolated)
Farewell in God the Father, and in Jesus Christ, our common hope (*Ephesians* 21).	Fare ye well in God the Father, and the Lord Jesus Christ, our common hope, and in the Holy Ghost.
Ye who have obtained the inseparable Spirit, who is Jesus Christ (*Magnesians* 15).	Ye who have obtained the inseparable Spirit, in Christ Jesus, by the will of God.
Fare ye well in the grace of God (*Smyrnaeans* 13).	Fare ye well in the grace of God, and of our Lord Jesus Christ, being filled with the Holy Spirit.

The following phrases show that Ignatius identified Jesus as the one God manifested in flesh. By contrast, in the third century, trinitarians such as Origen objected to the practice of calling Jesus God without qualification. In several of these passages, Ignatius specifically identified Jesus as the indwelling Holy Spirit. Assuming Ignatius understood God to be the Father (as stated in such verses as John 17:3, I Corinthians 8:6, II Corinthians 1:2-3, and Ephesians 4:6), he thought of Jesus as God the Father incarnate.

Epistle to the Ephesians: "Jesus Christ, our God" (salutation). "Jesus Christ, our inseparable life, is the (manifested) will of the Father" (3). (Richardson's translation says, "Jesus Christ . . . is the Father's mind.") "[Jesus] may be in us as our God, which indeed He is, and will manifest Himself before our faces" (15). "We have received the knowledge of God, which is Jesus Christ" (17). "Our God, Jesus Christ, was according to the appointment of God, conceived in the womb of Mary, of the seed of David, but by the Holy Ghost" (18). "God Himself being manifested in human form" (19).

Epistle to the Magnesians: "There is one God, who has manifested Himself by Jesus Christ His Son, who is His eternal Word" (8). (Lightfoot's translation says God manifested Himself "through" Jesus Christ.[5]) "The inseparable Spirit, who is Jesus Christ" (15).

Epistle to the Trallians: "Jesus Christ our God" (7).

Epistle to the Romans: "Jesus Christ our God" (salutation). "The passion [suffering] of my God" (6).

Epistle to the Smyrnaeans: "I glorify God, even Jesus Christ" (1). (The long version says, "I glorify the God and Father of our Lord Jesus Christ.") "He that is among the wild beasts is in company with God; provided only he be so in the name of Jesus Christ" (4). Chapter 10 speaks of servants of "Christ our God," literally, "the Christ God," but the altered version says simply "the servants of Christ."

Epistle to Polycarp: "Look for Him who is above all time, eternal and invisible, yet who became visible for our sakes; impalpable and impassible, yet who became passible on our account; and who in every kind of way suffered for our sakes" (3). "Our God, Jesus Christ" (8).

Ephesians 7 describes Jesus Christ as the one God who suffered in the flesh: "There is one Physician who is possessed both of flesh and spirit; both made and not made; God existing in flesh; true life in death; both of Mary and of God; first passible and then impassible—even Jesus Christ our Lord." Tertullian later ridiculed the modalists for this very teaching. Fourth-century trinitarian scribes apparently recognized the "heresy" of *Ephesians* 7 and changed it, for the long version reads, "We have also as a Physician the Lord our God, Jesus the Christ, the only-begotten Son and Word, before time began, but who afterwards became also man, of Mary the virgin. For 'the Word was made flesh.' Being incorporeal, He was in the body; being impassible, He was in a passible body; being immortal, He was in a mortal body."

For Ignatius, Christians are people of the name of Jesus, which is the revealed name of God. "I came bound from Syria for the common name" (*Ephesians* 1). "I am bound for the name (of Christ)" (3). "Some are in the habit of carrying about the name (of Jesus Christ) in wicked guile" (7). "The grace that we owe to the Name" (20, Richardson). "The church which . . . is named from Christ, and from the Father" (*Romans*, salutation), or "being true to Christ's law and stamped with the Father's name" (Richardson).

Only a few phrases of Ignatius could suggest trinitarianism, and these can be easily explained in a manner consistent with Oneness, much like threefold references in the New Testament. In a manner similar to II Corinthians 13:14 and I Peter 1:2, his *Ephesians* 9 speaks of God the Father, Jesus Christ, and the Holy Spirit to distinguish aspects of our salvation. Believers are described as stones "prepared for the building of God the Father, and drawn up on high by the instrument of Jesus Christ, which is the cross, making use of the Holy Spirit as a rope." In other words, believers are saved (prepared to be God's temple) through the atoning death of Jesus Christ, which is applied to individuals by the regenerating work of God's Spirit.

Magnesians 6 says Jesus was "with the Father before the beginning of time," which probably means in the sense of the eternal Word (John 1:1). The Greek for "with" here is *para* with the dative case, which, according to Thayer, "indicates that *something is* or is done either in the immediate vicinity of some one, or (metaph.) *in his mind.*"[6] Later scribes did not see this statement as definitely trinitarian, for they modified it to read, "He, being begotten by the Father before the beginning of time, was God the Word, the only-begotten Son."

Archbishop Wake's translation of Vossius's 1646 Greek text provides another reading of *Magnesians* 6 that is clearly Oneness: "Jesus Christ, who was the Father before all ages, and appeared in the end to us."[7] Since this reading fits better with the rest of Ignatius's statements, it seems likely that it is the original. If so, we can only speculate as to how many other similar statements by Ignatius or other early writers were deleted or altered.

Magnesians 7 and *Romans* 3 state that Jesus is "with" the Father. The editors note after the latter statement that an equally valid translation is "in" the Father.

This is the usual translation of the Greek preposition *en* here, and so Lightfoot translated the word.

Magnesians 13 is the only passage in Ignatius that speaks of Father, Son, and Spirit together. It exhorts believers to prosper in flesh and spirit, in faith and love, in Son, Father, and Spirit. It also tells them to be subject to the bishop and to one another as the apostles to Christ, the Father, and the Spirit and as Christ to the Father. In both places the threefold reference disrupts the pattern of twofold references.

We can explain these threefold references in terms of God's redemptive manifestations, but actually they seem to be additions. The longer version of the letter is actually shorter in this chapter, and it is apparently closer to the original words of Ignatius. It makes no mention of prospering in Father, Son, and Spirit, and it simply says to be subject to the bishop as Christ to the Father. This reading harmonizes better with the rest of the passage and with Ignatius's overall doctrine of God.

Fourth-century trinitarians apparently recognized how damaging the writings of Ignatius were to their cause and realized that none of the writings of this age clearly supported their doctrine. Consequently they interpolated Ignatius's epistles heavily and forged additional ones.

The false *Epistle to the Tarsians* tries to refute Ignatius's own doctrine, saying, "Certain of the ministers of Satan" wrongly assert that Jesus "is Himself God over all" (2). The writer continued, "He Himself is not God over all, and the Father, but His Son" (5).

The spurious *Epistle to the Philippians* likewise attempts to place trinitarian dogma and antimodalistic statements in the mouth of Ignatius. "There is then one

God and Father. . . . And there is also one Son, God the Word. . . . And there is also one Paraclete . . . . Not . . . one (person) having three names . . . but . . . three possessed of equal honour" (2). "For there is but One that became incarnate, and that neither the Father nor the Paraclete, but the Son only" (3). The writer denied that Christ is "God over all, and the Almighty" (7).

Scholars agree that these two epistles are fourth-century forgeries.

Polycarp

Polycarp left one brief *Epistle to the Philippians* (c. 112-18). He highly endorsed the letters of Ignatius, obviously agreeing with the doctrine of God expressed in them. "The Epistles of Ignatius written by him to us, and all the rest (of his Epistles) which we have by us, we have sent to you, as you requested. They are subjoined to this Epistle, and by them ye may be greatly profited" (13). Polycarp spoke of "God and our Lord" (1) and identified Jesus Christ as "our Lord and God" (6) and "the Son of God" (12).

The only passage that could imply trinitarianism is in chapter 12, which no longer exists in the original Greek; the only complete text is in Latin. According to it, Polycarp prayed that "the God and Father of our Lord Jesus Christ, and Jesus Christ Himself, who is the Son of God, and our everlasting High Priest, build you up in faith and truth" and asked for God's blessing on all who believe "in our Lord Jesus Christ, and in His Father, who raised him from the dead." This language is scriptural and makes a biblical distinction between God the Father and the man Jesus, who is our mediator and who died for us.

If Polycarp were trying to make a trinitarian statement here, it seems that he should have recognized the Holy Spirit as a third, coequal person by praying for His help also and by stating the need for faith in Him as well.

Polycarp died about 155. *The Martyrdom of Polycarp* by an unknown author can be no earlier, and some scholars date it much later. It is not a trustworthy eyewitness account, for it relates fanciful miracles: when Polycarp was burned at the stake, his body shone like gold and silver and gave off sweet odors, a dove flew out of his body, and his blood extinguished the fire. It contains many interpolations, as a comparison with a version preserved by Eusebius shows. It includes several trinitarian prayers, which are probably embellishments of the original story or interpolations. They exist in contradictory forms, and scholars have noted that they sound remarkably like "Eucharistic prayers of a later date."[8]

For example, Polycarp's prayer, which scholars generally agree is fictitious or heavily interpolated, gives glory to God "along with" Jesus Christ and "to" the Holy Ghost (14). Eusebius's version gives glory to God with Jesus Christ "in the Holy Ghost." The account also says that Polycarp glorified God the Father and blessed Jesus Christ (19); later manuscripts add a blessing to the Holy Spirit. The closing salutation twice gives glory to Jesus Christ, God the Father, and the Holy Spirit. A scribe named Pionius added the second statement of praise, and an earlier scribe probably added or embellished the first.

Hermas

The Shepherd of Hermas (or *The Pastor*) (c. 140-45) was written by an unknown man named Hermas in Rome.

The date makes it impossible for him to be the Hermas mentioned in Romans 16:14, as some supposed. The *Muratorian Fragment (c.* 170) says he was the brother of Pius, bishop of Rome, and that he had recently written *The Shepherd.* This work was quite popular in ancient Christendom.

The Shepherd affirms that God is one: "First of all, believe that there is one God who created and finished all things" (Commandment 1).

One passage may imply a preexistent Son as a separate person: "The Son of God is older than all His creatures, so that He was a fellow-councillor with the Father in His work of creation" (Similitude 9:12). Hermas may have meant simply that the Son existed in the plan and mind of God, however, for he also called the church "an old woman . . . because . . . she was created first of all. On this account is she old. And for her sake was the world made" (Vision 2:4). *II Clement,* an anonymous sermon written about the same time, similarly describes the church as preexistent in the plan of God. (See chapter 3.)

Another passage in Hermas describes the flesh of Jesus Christ as indwelt by the Holy Spirit and as the partner of the Holy Spirit. It then says, "For this conduct of the flesh pleased Him [God], because it was not defiled on the earth while having the Holy Spirit. He took, therefore, as fellow-councillors His Son and the glorious angels" (Sim. 5:6). The text here is somewhat uncertain and obscure, as the editors note, but it seems to identify the Son with the flesh of Christ (indwelt by the Holy Spirit) and to identify the time that the Son was a counsellor with the Incarnation. Perhaps Hermas spoke of the

Son as God's counsellor in creation because God created humanity with the Son in view, in dependence upon the manifestation of the future Son of God to redeem fallen humanity and recreate believers spiritually. (See Hebrews 1:1-3.)

Elsewhere the book equates the Father with the Lord (Vis. 3:9).

Hermas did not see the Holy Spirit as a separate person of the Godhead but said He was manifested to the world as the Son: "The holy, pre-existent Spirit, that created every creature, God made to dwell in flesh, which He chose. This flesh, accordingly, in which the Holy Spirit dwelt, was nobly subject to that Spirit" (Sim. 5:6). (An alternate text says here, "The Holy Spirit, who created all things, dwelt in a body in which He wished to dwell.") "I wish to explain to you what the Holy Spirit . . . showed you, for that Spirit is the Son of God (Sim. 9: 1). [Ye] will dwell with the Son of God; for ye have received of His Spirit" (Sim. 9:24). "The man being filled with the Holy Spirit, speaks to the multitude as the Lord wishes. Thus, then, will the Spirit of Divinity become manifest. Whatever power therefore comes from the Spirit of Divinity belongs to the Lord" (Com. 11).

Hermas taught the essentiality of water baptism, the name of God, the Holy Spirit, and holiness of life. He alluded to the Jesus Name formula, stating that Christians receive the Lord's name at water baptism: "Your life has been, and will be, saved through water . . . founded on the word of the almighty and glorious Name" (Vis. 3:3). "These are they who have heard the word, and wish to be baptized in the name of the Lord" (Vis. 3:7). "The name of the Lord by which they were called" (Sim. 8:6). "No one shall enter into the kingdom of God unless he receive His holy name. . . . A man cannot otherwise enter into the kingdom of God than by the name of His beloved Son. . . . Whosoever does not receive His name, shall not enter into the kingdom of God" (Sim. 9:12). "If you bear His name but possess not His power, it will be in vain that you bear His name" (Sim. 9:13). "The name of the Son of God is great, and cannot be contained, and supports the whole world" (Sim. 9:14). "Before a man bears the name of the Son of God he is dead; but when he receives the seal he lays aside his deadness, and obtains life. The seal, then, is the water: they descend into the water dead and they arise alive" (Sim. 9:16). "Ye who suffer for His name ought to glorify God, because He deemed you worthy to bear His name, that all your sins might be healed" (Sim. 9:28). This last statement is a reference to baptism, for Hermas taught that remission of sins comes only by water baptism (Com. 4:3).

Conclusions

The writings of Clement of Rome, Ignatius, Polycarp, and Hermas adhere closely to biblical language, usage, and thought. These writers affirmed that God is one, that Jesus Christ is the true God, and that Christ is truly human. They distinguished between God and Jesus Christ in the sense that the New Testament does, distinguishing Father and Son, the eternal Spirit and the man Christ through whom God manifested Himself. They did not see a distinction with regard to the Holy Spirit. To them the Holy Spirit was the Spirit of the one God and was Jesus Christ Himself in Spirit form. They attached great significance to the name of God and alluded to baptism in the name of Jesus. On all these points they exhibit a close affinity to modern Oneness.

Some trinitarians have objected that these writers did not explicitly identify Jesus as the Father incarnate, as modern Oneness does. It appears that Ignatius in fact did so. In addition, Clement and Polycarp identified Jesus as the one God in the biblical sense, which strongly implies that He is the Father incarnate, and they interchanged titles for the Father and Jesus. Moreover, in Scripture, the primary use of the title of Father is to distinguish God from His Son, the man Christ in whom God was incarnate, and the early post-apostolic writers simply continued that usage. Oneness writers today do so as well, but because of trinitarian error on this point, they often explain that for Jesus to be God incarnate actually means that He is the Father incarnate.

Clement, Ignatius, Polycarp, and Hermas did not describe God as a trinity or as three persons, nor did they use any other distinctively trinitarian language. Some of their statements are incompatible with trinitarianism, ancient and modern, and many sound like Oneness expressions today. (Later, in fact, trinitarian copyists were frequently uncomfortable with the language of Ignatius in particular and attempted to correct it.) Trinitarian phrases are absent where they would be most expected and even required, such as in prayers, statements of praise to God, closing benedictions, and references to baptism. If the early Christians embraced trinitarianism, which contrasts sharply with Old Testament monotheism as taught by the Judaism from which they had recently emerged, and if such belief were essential to salvation as trinitarians later asserted, then we would expect these early writers to emphasize this doctrine heavily. That they did not is highly significant.

The monotheistic, biblical, nontrinitarian character of their writings is particularly evident when we contrast them with later second-century and early third-century writers, who used philosophical terms and ideas heavily and who emphasized that God exists as a plurality of number (Justin), Gods (Justin and Origen), "persons" (Tertullian and Origen), "beings" (Tertullian and Origen), "entities" (Origen), and "individuals" (Hippolytus).

Oneness believers can easily embrace the language of the church leaders whose writings we have, namely, the bishops Clement, Ignatius, Polycarp, and (as we shall see in chapter 3) Papias. The allegedly trinitarian phrases are few, ambiguous, and offhand, and they can easily be interpreted in a nontrinitarian way.

Some trinitarians claim that the very casualness of these supposedly trinitarian references demonstrates that the doctrine of the trinity was deeply ingrained in the writers and commonly assumed. Therefore, they say, trinitarianism was presumed instead of taught, and it popped out in contexts where it would not necessarily be expected. This argument is not plausible in light of the subsequent centuries of bitter controversy over trinitarianism and the difficulty with which it was defined. Rather, the scarcity of these references and the offhand nature of them indicate that the authors attached no special significance to them. Since they predated the formulation of trinitarian dogma, these phrases were not as confusing or ambiguous as they might appear today. There was no potential for them to be interpreted in a trinitarian fashion when they were written; the people of the age simply did not think in such categories.

The only really questionable statements appear in the writing of the unknown Hermas. His work contains a few unclear statements that possibly refer to a preexistent Son, but it poses at least as many problems for trinitarians as for Oneness adherents. For example, it equates Jesus with the Holy Spirit. At most, it indicates a doctrine of two persons, one subordinate to the other, and not a trinity of coequal persons.

We cannot call these writers antitrinitarians, for the doctrine of the trinity had not yet been formulated. Hermas may have adhered to a vague, undefined form of binitarianism (belief in two persons), but the others, including the church leaders of the time, simply did not think in trinitarian terms. Their doctrine of God was Christocentric (centered around Christ) and monotheistic (affirming that God is one). It was much more biblical and much less philosophical than trinitarianism is. In sum, these writings correspond closely to modern Oneness. They are certainly much closer to Oneness than to trinitarianism in any form.

3

Anonymous and Pseudonymous Writings

Chapter 2 discussed the major writers of the Post-Apostolic Age, but our study would not be complete without looking at the other writings that survive from that time, namely, the *Didache*, the *Second Epistle of Clement*, the *Epistle of Barnabas*, the *Preaching of Peter*, and fragments from Papias, bishop of Hierapolis.

With the exception of Papias, the authors of these writings are unknown. The author or authors of the *Didache*, or *Teaching of the Twelve Apostles*, are anonymous. Historians agree that the *Didache* was not written by the apostles or endorsed by them in any way, despite the claim of its title. The other three works bear the names of Clement, Barnabas, and Peter, but historians agree that the prominent church leaders who bore these names did not write them. Either the authors used these pseudonyms to facilitate the reception of their writings, which casts doubt on their credibility, or else scribes later wrongly attributed the works to famous historical figures.

Only the *Didache*, *II Clement*, and *Barnabas* contain statements relevant to our investigation. Evidently the authors were not prominent in their day and did not hold significant positions in the church, or else they would have relied upon their own names and offices to establish the credibility of their writings. They are unknown at best and deceptive at worst. Consequently, we have little assurance that they spoke with authority in their day. Except when we find corroboration in other sources, there is little justification to regard a particular view in these writings as representative of the church of their time. In addition, the *Didache* and *II Clement* may actually have originated after the Post-Apostolic Age in the middle to latter part of the second century. In sum, these writings reveal thoughts current in the early second century, but it is not clear how prevalent or accepted some of these ideas were.

The "Didache"

For our purposes, the most significant passage of the *Didache*, or *Teaching of the Twelve Apostles*, is its description of the baptismal formula. Since one passage mentions, in its present form at least, a threefold baptismal formula, many trinitarians today appeal to it as a trinitarian document, and some of them even place it in the first century. A study of this document, however, leads to the following conclusions: (1) The *Didache* is not a first-century document. (2) It is not a reliable representative of the early church. (3) It does not teach trinitarianism.

Opponents of Oneness usually propose an extremely early date for the *Didache*. For example, E. Calvin Beisner, a former associate of the late Walter Martin, wrote in a letter dated October 24, 1988:

The *Didache*, the earliest extant piece of Christian literature outside the New Testament itself, . . .

cannot have originated later than the end of the first century or the earliest decade or two of the second, and . . . based on internal and external evidence, probably originated between A.D. 35 and 60 (and thus predates even some New Testament writings).

His book, *God in Three Persons*, dates the *Didache* to A.D. 35-60.[1] Similarly, Jim Beverley wrote, "The earliest Christian writing (the *Didache)* has trinitarian overtones."[2]

Most scholars today, however, maintain that the *Didache* is a second-century document. The definition in *Webster's New World Dictionary* reflects this consensus: "an anonymous Christian treatise of the early 2nd cent." Cyril Richardson, editor and translator of *Early Christian Fathers*, explained, "At one time this tract was viewed as a very ancient product—as early as A.D. 70 or 90. Recent study, however, has conclusively shown that, in the form we have it, it belongs to the second century."[3]

M. B. Riddle gave a similar explanation in *The Ante-Nicene Fathers*, the most widely used compilation of the early Christian writings in English.

It seems on many accounts improbable that the work, in its present form, was written earlier than the beginning of the second century. . . . Bryennios and Harnack assign, as the date, between 120 and 160; Hilgenfeld, 160 and 190; English and American scholars vary between A.D. 80 and 120. Until the priority to Barnabas is more positively established, the two may be regarded as of the same age, about 120, although a date slightly later is not impossible.[4]

The idea that the *Didache* is "the earliest Christian writing" is incredible. At least twenty-seven documents have prior claim to that title: the books of the New Testament itself.

The date 35-60 is likewise untenable. The *Didache* refers repeatedly to passages from the Gospel of Matthew, which was written about 66-68. (See, for example, *Didache* 1, 8, and 15.) It contains at least one unmistakable reference to the Book of Revelation, which was written about 95-96. (Compare *Didache* 16:4 with Revelation 12:9.) Scholars such as Lange, Alford, Elliott, Godet, Lee, Milligan, Hiebert, Morris, Wilbur Smith, and others say the Book of Revelation was written in the latter part of the reign of the emperor Domitian (81-96), based on both early tradition and internal considerations (such as the condition of the seven churches). Early writers uniformly testified that Domitian banished John to Patmos, and some said he did so in 95.

If the *Didache* were a first-century document that accurately summarized apostolic teaching and had apostolic authority, as its name implies, then surely it would have been included in the New Testament. Other books meeting those criteria were, even some that were not written by apostles (Mark, Luke, James, Jude) and one whose authorship is uncertain (Hebrews).

Aside from the question of the date, it is amazing that some trinitarians are willing to rely so heavily upon the *Didache*. If they use it to show that the original baptismal formula was trinitarian, they may in effect give it priority over the clear historical statements of the Book of Acts and the teachings of the Epistles. This is tantamount to establishing doctrine on the basis of extrabiblical authority.

Only one Greek manuscript of the *Didache* exists today. It was discovered in 1873, and it is dated 1056. (There are also some references to the *Didache* in writings of church fathers, and we have a fragment of a tenth-century Latin translation that contains many textual variations.) Apparently, Christians of the first few centuries did not consider this work important enough to make many copies of it, to circulate it widely, or to take great care for its preservation.

Scholars agree that the apostles did not write the *Didache*. They commonly propose a composite authorship and suggest that the authors were not necessarily representative of Christianity of that day. In this regard, Riddle stated:

> The work represents, on many of these points, only a very small fraction of the Christians during the second century, and . . . while it casts some light upon usages of that period, it cannot be regarded as an authoritative witness concerning the universal faith and practice of believers at the date usually assigned to it. The few notices of it, and its early disappearance, confirm this position. The theory of a composite origin also accords with this estimate of the document as a whole.[5]

Richardson likewise described the uncertainty and unreliability of the text:

> [It] is the first of those fictitious Church Orders which edit ancient material and claim apostolic authorship. As in many such instances . . . we cannot be sure precisely what is original and what is edited. . . .

Sometimes a scribe will brush up ancient material sufficiently to make it appear relevant to his period. More often he will change it only a little, leaving a curious combination of the ancient and the modern, which is bewildering.[6]

These comments suggest that the text contains many interpolations. It is likely that changes were made in the approximately nine hundred years between the original and our only copy. Riddle noted, "Owing to an absence of other copies, we cannot determine the purity of the text; but there is every probability of many minor corruptions."[7] And these changes would tend to reflect the dominant doctrines of the intervening time—those of Roman Catholicism.

It is evident that the *Didache is* not a reliable source for apostolic doctrines and practices, for it mentions several that are clearly of postbiblical origin, particularly with respect to baptism. For example, chapter 7, the chapter that refers to a threefold baptismal formula, teaches several other nonbiblical practices: the baptizer and candidate must fast one or two days before baptism; baptism should be in running, cold water if possible; if immersion is not possible, water should be poured on the head three times.

Although the *Didache* is supposed to summarize the essential Christian teachings, it does not teach trinitarianism. Its Eucharistic prayers address the Father alone, describing Him as Master, Lord, and Creator, giving all glory to Him, and thanking Him for His Servant Jesus Christ (9, 10). By contrast, trinitarian Eucharistic prayers address the Father, Son, and Holy Spirit. Chapter 10 says, "Hosanna to the God of David," thereby identifying Jesus the Messiah as the God of the Old Testament.

The only possible trinitarian reference is the baptismal formula. As the *Encyclopedia of Religion and Ethics* indicates, however, scholars generally date the first mention of a threefold formula to Justin about 150 rather than to the *Didache*.[8]

The *Didache* says to "baptize into the name of the Father, and of the Son, and of the Holy Spirit, in living water" (7:1). But it also says, "Let no one eat or drink of your Thanksgiving (Eucharist), but they who have been baptized into the name of the Lord," and the same passage identifies the Lord as Jesus (9:5). Interestingly, 10:2 describes Christians as bearing the singular name of the Father: "We thank Thee, holy Father, for Thy holy name which Thou didst cause to tabernacle in our hearts."

We can explain the apparent contradiction between 7:1 and 9:5 in several ways. (1) Trinitarians often say that 7:1 quotes the exact baptismal formula, while 9:5 refers to Christ's authority. The grammatical construction is identical in both places, however. They ignore the obvious parallel to the Book of Acts, where the Jesus Name formula appears. (2) Both are an indirect reference to the Jesus Name formula, much as Matthew 28:19 and Acts 10:48 (KJV). Perhaps the original author simply quoted Matthew 28:19. (3) The two statements are contradictory. This could be true if the document was composed by different people, by someone who wished to change the baptismal practice, or by a compromiser. (4) One of the passages has been altered, which is probable in light of later doctrinal deviations.

Apostolic Constitutions 7:22, a fourth-century adaptation of *Didache* 7, supports the idea that the latter was originally a simple quotation of Matthew 28:19

later expanded to teach the trinitarian formula and triple baptism. *Constitutions* 7:22 actually quotes Matthew 28:19 and then describes baptism as a burial with Christ, with no mention of triple baptism. It is also interesting to note that *Constitutions* 8:44 addresses "every lay Christian, upon whom the name of our Lord Jesus Christ is called."

If copyists altered a passage, then 7:1 was changed or inserted rather than 9:5, for the original baptismal formula as stated in Acts was Jesus Name. The *Encyclopedia of Religion and Ethics* states that perhaps 7:1 originally read "in the name of the Lord" like 9:5.[9] If a copyist wanted to "clarify" or "correct" the *Didache's* teaching on baptism, he would certainly change the baptismal instructions, but he might not notice the significance of the baptismal reference in the Eucharistic section.

Significantly, *Constitutions* 7:25, which is an expansion of *Didache* 9:5, eliminates "name" totally: "Let no one eat of these things that is not initiated; but those only who have been baptized into the death of the Lord." Apparently the fourth-century writer, aware of the controversies over the baptismal formula and the Godhead, became uncomfortable with the Jesus Name phrase and decided to "explain" it.

A later writer was uncomfortable even with the altered phrase. The last canon of the *Constitutions* in the collection of Dionysius, which is of later origin, requires triple immersion into three titles, "for the Lord did not say, 'Baptize into my death'" (8:47). John of Antioch's collection adds here a denunciation of modalism, including any belief "that names the Holy Spirit Father or Son" or "that there is one God with three names."

Based on the preceding evidence, we deduce the following: (1) *Didache* 9:5 is an authentic reference to the original Jesus Name formula. (2) *Didache* 7:1 is a doctrinal corruption. Perhaps the original writer wrongly accepted the trinitarian formula; perhaps he simply quoted Matthew 28:19 and copyists later altered his words somewhat; or, most probably, the phrase in question has been changed or inserted. (3) *Apostolic Constitutions* 7:25 is a later effort to remove all traces of the original formula.

"II Clement"

The so-called *Second Epistle of Clement is* an ancient sermon by an unknown author. Lightfoot dated it 120-40, and some scholars have dated it as early as 100, but most scholars today say it was written around 150.

This sermon emphasizes the identity of Jesus as the one God, our Father. "It is fitting that you should think of Jesus Christ as of God. . . . As a Father, He has called us sons. He has saved us" (1).

The author thought of God as one, making no references to indicate a plurality of divine persons. He concluded by saying, "To the only God, invisible, the Father of truth, who send forth to us the Saviour and Prince of incorruption, through whom He also manifested to us the truth and the heavenly life, to Him be the glory for ever and ever" (20). By identifying the Father as the only God and by identifying Jesus as God and Father, this sermon indicates that Jesus is the Father incarnate.

The work also incorporates the doctrine of the name of God. It admonishes Christians to be holy so "that the Name be not blasphemed on account of us" (13).

Like Ignatius and Hermas, the author taught that as to His deity Jesus is the Holy Spirit. Apparently, this identification was standard in the Post-Apostolic Age. "Christ the Lord who saved us, though He was first a Spirit, became flesh" (9). "The Church is not of the present, but from the beginning. For she was spiritual, as our Jesus also was, but was manifested in the last days that He might save us. . . . But if we say that the flesh is the Church and the spirit Christ, then he that hath shamefully used the flesh hath shamefully used the Church. Such a one then shall not partake of the spirit, which is Christ. Such life and incorruption this flesh can partake of, when the Holy Spirit is joined to it" (14).

Some trinitarians explain that *II Clement* merely identifies Jesus as a spirit being, not as the Holy Spirit. For this reason, it seems, the translators used "spirit" instead of "Spirit" in the foregoing quotation from chapter 14. But the immediate context of this passage shows otherwise. Both before and after the identification of Jesus as the Spirit, the author spoke of the Holy Spirit.

This passage parallels Hermas by identifying Jesus as the Spirit and by speaking of the church as preexistent (in the plan of God). It thereby lends support to the idea that when Hermas spoke of the preexistence of the Son he meant that the Son preexisted in the mind of God with respect to His humanity and as the one eternal Spirit with respect to His deity, rather than as a second person.

Pseudo-Barnabas

The author of the so-called *Epistle of Barnabas* (c. 100-20) is not the Barnabas of the New Testament but an unknown person. No one before Clement of Alexandria ascribed this work to Barnabas, and Eusebius listed it as spurious. E. H. Klotsche suggested that since "its method is extremely Alexandrine" it was probably written by "a converted Jew from Alexandria."[10]

The significance of this writing for our subject is its assertion that when God said, "Let us make man" in Genesis 1:26, He spoke to the "Lord of all the world" (5), or to "the Son" (6). These statements appear in the context of explaining New Testament salvation, not the Godhead. Although the author's precise meaning is unclear, perhaps he meant that God looked forward in time to the redemptive work of the Son, much as we suggested for Hermas.

Lightfoot's translation shows that this interpretation is most likely: "Forasmuch then as He [the Lord] renewed us in the remission of sins, He made us to be a new type . . . as if He were re-creating us. For the scripture saith concerning us, how He saith to the Son; Let us make man after our image and after our likeness." Following the Latin version, the rendering of *The Ante-Nicene Fathers* says this work of re-creating occurs by the operation of the Spirit: "He has created us anew by His Spirit."

Later trinitarians used this statement to teach a pre-existent, coexistent Son, but it is not clear that the author had these later connotations in mind. In the same context, he defined the Son primarily in terms of the Incarnation, saying that the Lord "manifested Himself to be the Son of God. . . . The Son of God therefore came in the flesh" (5).

Papias and "Preaching of Peter"

The fragments of Papias (c. 125) and the spurious *Preaching of Peter* (c. 110-30) contain nothing of significance to our discussion. *The Ante-Nicene Fathers* includes in the fragments of Papias this statement: "[We] ascend through the Spirit to the Son, and through the Son to the Father." Irenaeus quoted the paragraph containing this sentence from "the presbyters," and the editors admitted that it was a "mere guess" to say it comes from Papias. Lightfoot did not include the passage in the fragments of Papias.

The phrase can be interpreted as referring either to three divine persons or to three manifestations of God for our redemption. It could be an allusion to Ignatius's statement in *Ephesians* 9, in which case the latter view would seem to apply. Since the actual wording comes from Irenaeus, the phrase is more indicative of his theology than anyone else's.

Conclusions

For the most part these writings confirm the conclusions of chapter 2 regarding the doctrine of God in the Post-Apostolic Age. Once again, we find affirmations of God's oneness, the absolute deity of Jesus Christ, and the significance of the name of God. The Son of God is distinguished from God as to His humanity. The Spirit of God is not distinguished from God and is identified with Jesus Christ. In particular, *II Clement* expresses characteristic Oneness beliefs.

There are no clear trinitarian statements in these writings and no distinctively trinitarian terminology. If we accept an early date for the *Didache* and if we accept the present text of *Didache* 7:1, then sometime during this age a threefold baptismal formula began to emerge. Even so, Lutheran professor Otto Heick set the earliest date for general acceptance of the trinitarian formula at about 130 to 140.[11] More probably, the baptismal formula in *Didache* 7:1 is an interpolation and acceptance of such a formula came significantly later. (See chapters 4 and 8.)

Questionable statements relative to the Son appear in the work of Pseudo-Barnabas. It is not clear exactly what he meant, but perhaps he thought of the Son as preexistent in some manner distinct from God Himself. If so, he leaned toward a form of binitarianism, similar to the later doctrine of the Greek Apologists.

In surveying the Post-Apostolic Age, Oneness adherents find questionable statements relative to the doctrine of God only in works by authors who are otherwise unknown and who evidently held no significant position in the church: Hermas, the author(s) of the *Didache*, and Pseudo-Barnabas.

The problems that trinitarians must face in these writings are much greater. Bishop Ignatius, Hermas, and the author of *II Clement* all contradicted trinitarianism by identifying Jesus as the Holy Spirit. The author of *II Clement* and, apparently, Bishop Ignatius identified Jesus as Father. Bishops Clement and Ignatius spoke of God's suffering in a way that third-century trinitarians such as Tertullian condemned, Bishop Polycarp heartily endorsed all the writings of Ignatius, and all three bishops spoke of Jesus as God in an unqualified way that third-century trinitarians such as Origen opposed.

The
Age of the Greek Apologists,
A.D. 130-180

4

Justin

The writings of the Greek Apologists are significantly different from the writings of the Post-Apostolic Age. The writers of the Post-Apostolic Age addressed Christians, while the Apologists wrote to non-Christians. The most influential writers of the earlier age were bishops; the most influential Apologists were philosophers who apparently had no significant leadership position in the church. The earlier writers adhered more closely to biblical language and thought, while the Apologists were more philosophical and speculative. In particular, as chapter 1 has discussed, the Apologists employed Greek philosophical ideas and terms to explain and defend Christianity. In doing so, they introduced several innovations, the most important of which was their doctrine of the Word (Logos).

By far the most significant Greek Apologist was Flavius Justinus, or Justin, who was born in a Roman colony in Samaria. He was a Greek philosopher who continued to wear the philosopher's cloak and title after his conversion to Christianity. Justin was not ordained and did not hold a church office but was an itinerant lay teacher. At two different times he resided in Rome, where he was beheaded for his beliefs. He has traditionally been surnamed Philosopher and Martyr.[1]

Justin's existing writings are more voluminous than all the others of this period combined, and he influenced later writers heavily. More than any other, he is responsible for the second-century doctrine of the Logos.

The Logos doctrine was the Apologists' most significant innovation. The concept of the Logos ("Word") was very popular in Hellenistic culture. In Greek philosophy, the Logos meant reason, particularly as the controlling principle of the universe. The Greek philosopher Plato taught that there are two worlds: the good, real world of ideas or forms and the imperfect, physical world of phenomena that reflects the world of ideas. The summit of the world of ideas is the one supreme, perfect God, who is uninvolved with the evil world of matter and who is impassible (incapable of emotional feeling and suffering). Thus the world of ideas serves as an intermediary between God and the physical world.

The Hellenistic Jewish philosopher Philo of Alexandria, a contemporary of Jesus, applied these Greek ideas to the Old Testament by identifying the Logos with God's word and wisdom. He described the Logos as the instrument of creation and the intermediary between God and humanity, and he called the Logos the son of God, first-begotten of God, and second God. He did not attribute to the Logos distinct personality, however.[2]

The Gospel of John uses the term in a different way to explain God's manifestation in flesh as Jesus Christ. It does not separate the Logos from God but teaches the eternity of the Logos and identifies the Logos with God Himself, using the term to mean the expression of God's eternal mind and plan and God's self-revelation in flesh (John 1:1, 14).

Edward Hardy explained how Justin took the Greek idea of the Logos, altered it, and incorporated it into Christianity:

> The idea of God's Logos could be found in a variety of sources. It was floating in the air of popular Greek philosophy and Hellenistic Judaism. . . . (The chief thing to remember about the word "logos" is that it means everything except a single word—speech, design, argument, reason—therefore God's thought, plan, utterance, and so on.) Justin's use of it is partly Biblical and partly apologetic. The Logos being divine, and yet not the Father himself, accounts both for the divinity which Christians have found in Jesus, and by retrospect for the divine appearances in the Old Testament.[3]

Let us examine the key features of Justin's doctrine of God.

Plurality in the Godhead

Justin's *First Apology* (c. 150) teaches a plurality in the Godhead. Justin acknowledged "the most true God, the Father of righteousness. . . . Both Him, and the Son (who came forth from Him and taught us these things, and the host of the other good angels who follow and are made like to Him), and the prophetic Spirit, we worship and adore" (6). "We reasonably worship [Jesus Christ], having learned that He is the Son of the true God Himself, and holding Him in the second place, and the prophetic

Spirit in the third" (13). At the Eucharistic celebration, the presiding brother "gives praise and glory to the Father of the universe, through the name of the Son and of the Holy Ghost" (65).

According to these passages, the Father is the true God. The Son and Spirit are secondary deities similar to angels. Although the point is somewhat obscured by the translators' artificial insertion of parentheses, chapter 6 speaks of the worship of angels on the same basis as worship of the Son and Spirit. Edward Hardy's translation in *Early Christian Fathers* says, "Him [God], and the Son who came from him, and taught us these things, and the array of the other good angels who follow him and are made like him, and the prophetic Spirit we worship and adore."[4]

The Word as a Subordinate Second Person

Justin equated the Son with the Word and distinguished the Word as a separate being from the Father. "For they who affirm that the Son is the Father, are proved neither to have become acquainted with the Father, nor to know that the Father of the universe has a Son; who also, being the first-begotten Word of God, is even God" (63). Apparently, he knew of people who identified the Father and Son as the same being, and he opposed them.

The Word was not a distinct person in eternity past but was generated by God before the creation of the world. "The Word . . . is the first-birth of God" (21). "The Word of God was born of God in a peculiar manner, different from ordinary generation" (22).

The *Second Apology* expresses the same concepts. "The Father . . . is unbegotten. . . . His Son, who alone is properly called Son, the Word, who also was with Him and was begotten before the works, when at first He created and arranged all things by Him, is called Christ" (6). "Next to God, we worship and love the Word who is from the unbegotten and ineffable God" (13).

Justin's *Dialogue with Trypho*, a Jew, states in strong terms that the Father and the Word are numerically distinct and that the Word is subordinate to the Father. The Son/Word is "another God." "There is . . . another God and Lord subject to the Maker of all things; who is also called an Angel, because He announces to men whatsoever the Maker of all things—above whom there is no other God—wishes to announce to them. . . . He who is said to have appeared to Abraham, and to Jacob, and to Moses, and who is called God, is distinct from Him who made all things—numerically, I mean, not (distinct) in will" (56). "God begat before all creatures a Beginning, (who was) a certain rational power (proceeding) from Himself, who is called by the Holy Spirit, now the Glory of the Lord, now the Son, again Wisdom, again an Angel, then God, and then Lord and Logos. . . . He was begotten of the Father by an act of will; just as we see happening among ourselves: for when we give out some word, we beget the word; yet not by abscission, so as to lessen the word (which remains) in us, when we give it out" (61).

Justin used Genesis 1:26 and 3:22 to demonstrate two divine beings (62) and said Genesis 19:24 "indicates that there were two in number" (129). According to him, all the Old Testament appearances of God to man were actually the Word (126), "for you must not imagine that the unbegotten God Himself came down or went up from any place. For the ineffable Father and Lord of all neither has come to any place, nor walks, nor sleeps, nor rises up, but remains in His own place, wherever that is" (127). He emphasized that the Father and the Word are "numerically distinct" (128, 129).

Justin opposed people in his day who taught that the Father and the Word were the same being, a form of Oneness belief. "They call Him the Word, because He carries tidings from the Father to men: but maintain that this power is indivisible and inseparable from the Father, just as they say that the light of the sun on earth is indivisible and inseparable from the sun in the heavens . . . so the Father, when He chooses, say they, causes His power to spring forth, and when He chooses, He makes it return to Himself" (128).

It is also interesting to note that according to Justin the Word taught wisdom to ancient Greek philosophers such as Socrates and Plato, who were thereby in a sense Christians before Christ (*Second Apology* 8, 10, 13).

Uncertain Doctrine of the Holy Spirit

Although Justin identified the Holy Spirit as a third being to worship, he did not distinguish the Spirit clearly from the Father and the Word or define the relationship among these three. Indeed, in several places he identified the Spirit as the Word.

For example, his *First Apology* frequently mentions the "prophetic Spirit" (6, 13) and says about Messianic passages in Isaiah that "God predicted [these things] by the Spirit of prophecy," but then it says "the prophets are inspired by the Divine Word" (33) and "the Divine Word" moved the prophets (36). Moreover, "it is wrong . . . to understand the Spirit and the power of God as anything else than the Word, who is also the first-born of God" (33), and in Messianic predictions "the Spirit of prophecy speaks from the person of Christ" (38).

A Modified Doctrine of the Name

It appears that Justin inherited the biblical doctrine of God's name as taught in the Post-Apostolic Age but modified it to fit his philosophical views. In accordance with the Greek concept of God as totally transcendent, he held that the name of God Himself is unknowable or inexpressible. "To the Father, who is unbegotten, there is no name given. . . . These words, Father, and God, and Creator, and Lord, and Master, are not names, but appellations derived from His good deeds and functions" (*Second Apology* 6). The passage then explains that Jesus, the Son's name "as man and Saviour," has great significance and power, so that "in the name of Jesus Christ" demons are cast out and people are healed.

Justin identified Jesus as the name by which God reveals Himself. "Moreover, in the book of Exodus we have also perceived that the name of God Himself, which He says, was not revealed to Abraham or to Jacob, was Jesus, and was declared mysteriously through Moses. . . . For the name of Him who said to Moses, 'for My name is in Him,' was Jesus" (*Dialogue* 85). He attached great import to the Old Testament name Joshua because it is equivalent to the name Jesus. He also found it highly significant that when the Philistines put the captured ark of the covenant on a cart, the cows pulling the cart went back to Israel to the field of a man named Joshua. "They were guided by the name of power [or, 'the power of the name']; just as formerly the people who survived of those that came out of Egypt, were guided into the land by him who had received the name Jesus (Joshua)" (132).

The *Hortatory Address to the Greeks*, which bears Justin's name, says, "God cannot be called by any proper name" (21). Some scholars say he wrote it; others say it is from his time but not by him. It repeatedly states that there is only one God (15-21) and identifies Him as the I AM who spoke to Moses (21).

A Threefold Baptismal Formula

Scholars generally say the first mention of a threefold baptismal formula occurs in Justin's *First Apology.* "In the name of God, the Father and Lord of the universe, and of our Saviour Jesus Christ, and of the Holy Spirit, [converts] then receive the washing with water. . . . In order that we . . . may obtain in the water the remission of sins formerly committed, there is pronounced over him who chooses to be born again, and has repented of his sins, the name of God the Father and Lord of the universe; he who leads to the laver the person that is to be washed calling him by this name alone. For no one can utter the name of the ineffable God; and if any one dare to say that there is a name, he raves with a hopeless madness. . . . And in the name of Jesus Christ . . . and in the name of the Holy Ghost . . . he who is illuminated is washed" (61).

While this is a threefold formula, it is not the modern trinitarian formula. First, it does not say "in the name of the Father, and of the Son, and of the Holy Spirit" but actually retains the name of Jesus Christ. Second, we have already seen that Justin did not regard Jesus and the Holy Spirit as coequal with the Father. Given his doctrine of God, clearly Justin's formula was not intended to confess the doctrine of the trinity that is considered orthodox today or to confess the full deity of Jesus Christ (even by trinitarian standards).

It appears that this formula was quite recent, for *The Shepherd* of Hermas, which was written only a few years earlier, was highly esteemed, and was widely distributed for many years, teaches the essentiality of the Jesus Name formula. Probably Justin himself or contemporaries who shared his doctrinal views initiated the trine (threefold) formula.

Since Justin held that the Father alone is the true, supreme God and that the Father is a numerically distinct being from Jesus, he was undoubtedly reluctant to practice the older form of baptism in the name of Jesus only. His theology dictated that he emphasize the Father at baptism, but the only scriptural justification he could find for doing so was Matthew 28:19, which also mentions the Son and Holy Ghost. This led Justin to use a trine formula, with the greatest emphasis placed upon the Father. Although elsewhere he admitted that *Father is* not really a name, he defended the invocation of this title on the ground that humanity has no other name by which to call God. His biting ridicule here suggests that he had strong opposition on this point. Evidently other people were teaching that Matthew 28:19 did not mean to invoke the title of Father but rather to invoke the one supreme name of God.

Justin retained the actual name of Jesus instead of the title of Son, apparently in deference to the original formula and perhaps to appease those who insisted upon using the name Jesus. Thus Justin's formula may actually have been a compromise halfway step from the original Jesus Name formula to the later trinitarian one. If so, it indirectly bears witness to the older Jesus Name formula. The new formula apparently arose because of a new view of plurality within the Godhead and a devaluation of the deity of Jesus Christ.

Much evidence indicates that the Jesus Name formula was still common in the third century and that general acceptance of a trine formula came significantly later than Justin's time. Cyprian said the followers of the heretic Marcion practiced baptism "in the name of Jesus Christ" *(Epistles* 72:4*)*. While Marcion's doctrine is false, the Jesus Name baptismal formula was apparently the standard one in use when the Marcionites broke away from the church around 144, and they maintained the original practice. Hippolytus revealed that many of the Montanists, a tongues-speaking group that began about 156 and split off from the mainstream church around 177, were modalists *(Refutation of All Heresies* 8:12); those who held such a view would not have used a trinitarian formula. The *Acts of Paul and Thecla,* probably written by an Asiatic presbyter in the second century, gives an account of baptism "in the name of Jesus Christ." Chapter 8 will present further evidence that the Jesus Name formula was prevalent and probably still dominant in the early third century.

Conclusions

In summary, Justin taught a plurality of divine persons or gods. He taught that the Son/Word is "another God" and "numerically distinct" from the Creator, the Father. It is not clear whether he thought of the Holy Spirit as a third divine person. Some passages imply that the Spirit is an angel, while others imply that the Spirit is the activity of the Word.

Justin clearly subordinated the Word to the Father as to power, authority, time, and substance. He said the Word is not eternal, is not equal to the Father, and is like an angel. In these statements we find the essential features of the later Arian doctrine (which the Council of Nicea condemned), although in a more moderate form.

Justin used a compromise threefold baptismal formula that included the name of Jesus. He partially retained the earlier emphasis on the name of God, believing that there was great power in the name of Jesus. He believed that water baptism was necessary for the remission of sins, and it is possible that he considered the name of Jesus to be significant in this regard. In any case, in the writings of Justin we have the first recorded threefold baptismal formula, which appeared in the second generation after the completion of the New Testament.

Chapter 5 will discuss the other Greek Apologists and draw further conclusions relative to the doctrine of God as expressed by the Apologists as a group, including Justin.

5

Other Writings of the Age

The other writers whose works survive from the age of the Greek Apologists were not nearly as prolific as Justin, and most of them were strongly influenced by him.

There were other important writers from this time who cannot be classified with the Greek Apologists. For example, Eusebius mentioned Hegesippus; Apolinarius, bishop of Hierapolis; and Dionysius, bishop of Corinth. Unfortunately, their works have not survived. (Apologists whose writings are also completely lost include Quadratus and Miltiades.) If we had them, especially the writings of church leaders, perhaps we would get a very different impression of this age.

As chapters 1 and 4 have discussed, the Greek Apologists wrote defenses of Christianity to nonbelievers, and they employed many ideas taken from Greek philosophy. In particular, their doctrine of the Word (Logos) was strongly influenced by Greek thought.

Aristides

Possibly the earliest existing apology is the *Apology* of Aristides. It dates to about 150, although some scholars say it was written as early as 125 or 130. Aristides was a philosopher in Athens who became a Christian.

We have only three manuscripts of his work: one in Syriac, one in Greek, and an Armenian fragment. The Greek text exists only in a somewhat modified form, incorporated in a fanciful tale called *The Life of Barlaam and Josaphat.*

The Syriac version expresses a biblical concept of the Son. "The Christians, then, trace the beginning of their religion from Jesus the Messiah; and he is named the Son of God Most High. And it is said that God came down from heaven, and from a Hebrew virgin assumed and clothed himself with flesh; and the Son of God lived in a daughter of man" (2). The parallel Greek text says the unbegotten God came down to reconcile the world to Himself: "Now the Christians trace their origin from the Lord Jesus Christ. And He is acknowledged by the Holy Spirit to be the Son of the most high God, who came down from heaven for the salvation of men. And being born of a pure virgin, unbegotten and immaculate, He assumed flesh and revealed himself among men that He might recall them to Himself from their wanderings after many gods" (15).

Aristides emphasized God's oneness. "God our Lord . . . is one, is all in all. . . . God is one in His nature. A single essence is proper to Him, since He is uniform in His nature and His essence" (Syriac, 13).

He explained the Jewish concept of God with approval and defined the Christian doctrine of God in a similar manner. "The Jews then say that God is one, the Creator of all, and omnipotent; and that it is not right that any other should be worshipped except this God alone. And herein they appear to approach the truth more than all the nations" (14). "For [the Christians] know and trust in God, the Creator of heaven and of earth, in whom and from whom are all things, to whom there is no other god as companion, from whom they received commandments which they engraved upon their minds and observe in hope and expectation of the world which is to come" (15). Interestingly, trinitarians such as Tertullian later condemned their opponents, the modalists, for having a Jewish doctrine of God.

The only possible trinitarian allusion in Aristides is the Greek parallel to the foregoing passage (confirmed by the Armenian fragment). "For [the Christians] know God, the Creator and Fashioner of all things through the only-begotten Son and the Holy Spirit; and beside Him they worship no other God. They have the commands of the Lord Jesus Christ Himself graven upon their hearts" (15). If this passage refers to some sort of trinity, however, it advocates worship of the Father alone and alludes to the Son and Spirit merely as His agents.

"Epistle to Diognetus"

Another early document from this period is the *Epistle to Diognetus*. Its author, date, and text are uncertain. Historians today usually date it at 150 or later, although some place it as early as 130. It exists only in copies of one medieval Greek manuscript that no longer exists. That manuscript ascribed authorship to Justin, but scholars today uniformly reject that claim.

The epistle describes the "God who gave His Son" as "our Nourisher, Father, Teacher, Counsellor, Healer, our Wisdom, Light, Honour, Glory, Power, and Life" (9). By contrast, third-century trinitarians associated some of these titles with the second and third persons of the trinity. For example, they used the title of Wisdom as a unique designation for the Son in contrast to the Father.

In several places this work uses a biblical definition of the Son as the revelation and incarnation of God Himself. "No man has either seen [God], or made Him known, but He has revealed Himself" (8). "He Himself took on Him the burden of our iniquities, He gave His own Son as a ransom for us" (9). "He sent the Word, that He might be manifested to the world. . . . This is He who was from the beginning, who appeared as if new, and was found old, and yet who is ever born afresh in the hearts of the saints. This is He who, being from everlasting, is to-day called the Son" (11).

Two passages, however, may indicate a preexistent Son distinct from God. "God Himself, who is almighty, the Creator of all things, and invisible, has sent from heaven, and placed among men, the truth, and the holy and incomprehensible Word, and has firmly established Him in their hearts. He [sent] . . . the very Creator and Fashioner of all things—by whom He made the heavens. . . . As a king sends his son, who is also a king, so sent He Him; as God He sent Him" (7). "He formed in His mind a great and unspeakable conception, which He communicated to His Son alone. . . . After He revealed and laid open, through His beloved Son, the things which had been prepared from the beginning, He conferred every blessing all at once upon us. . . . He was aware, then, of all things in His own mind, along with His Son, according to the relation subsisting between them" (8).

Tatian

Justin's disciple Tatian expressed concepts quite similar to his teacher in his *Address to the Greeks* (c.

150). Originally, God the Father existed alone. "Our God did not begin to be in time: He alone is without beginning, and He Himself is the beginning of all things. God is a Spirit. . . . He is invisible, impalpable, being Himself the Father of both sensible and invisible things" (4).

The Logos was originally an impersonal power inherent in the Father, but before creation the Logos was "begotten" or "emanated" from the Father as a distinct being. "God was in the beginning; but the beginning, we have been taught, is the power of the Logos. . . . With Him, by Logos-power, the Logos Himself also, who was in Him, subsists. And by His simple will the Logos springs forth; and the Logos, not coming forth in vain, becomes the first-begotten work of the Father. Him (the Logos) we know to be the beginning of the world. . . . So the Logos, coming forth from the Logos–power of the Father, has not divested of the Logos–power Him who begat Him. I myself, for instance, talk, and you hear; yet, certainly, I who converse do not become destitute of speech (*logos*) by the transmission of speech, but by the utterance of my voice I endeavour to reduce to order the unarranged matter in your minds. . . . The Logos, begotten in the beginning, begat in turn our world" (5). "The heavenly Logos [was] a spirit emanating from the Father and a Logos from the Logos-power" (7).

Since Tatian held that the Logos was originally inherent in the Father, his *Diatessaron* rendered the last phrase of John 1:1 as, "God is the Word" (1). In effect, he interpreted John 1:1 much as Oneness believers do today. As far as eternity past is concerned he apparently had a Oneness concept. He differed from Oneness in teaching that at a certain point in time before the creation of the world the Word came out of God as a distinct person.

Melito

Melito, bishop of Sardis, was an influential writer of the time, but only fragments of his works survive. These fragments contain a number of statements that are reminiscent of the writings of the Post-Apostolic Age and that are similar to the teachings of the modalists. Perhaps his works did not survive because they contradicted the doctrine of God that became dominant. It would be particularly interesting to study his lost manuscript entitled *On God Incarnate.*

Melito's *Apology* (c. 170) emphasizes God's oneness and identifies God as the Father. "He, I say, really exists . . . and those who love Him speak of Him thus: 'Father, and God of Truth'. . . . God is One. . . . There is a God, the Father of all, who never came into being, neither was ever made, and by whose will all things subsist."

The Key says "the Lord" is the "Beginning and Creator of all things . . . the Ancient of Days" and then identifies the Lord as Jesus: "The transition of the Lord [is] His assumption of our flesh, through which by His birth, His death, His resurrection, His ascent into heaven, He made transitions." It describes the Son modalistically as "the mouth of the Lord, the word of the Lord, the arm of the Lord, the right hand of the Lord, the wisdom of the Lord." The Holy Spirit is similarly called "the tongue of the Lord, the finger of the Lord."

Several fragments identify Jesus as God in strong terms. The *Discourse on the Cross* says, "He was man . . . He is God; putting on the likeness of a servant, yet not impairing the likeness of His Father. He sustained every character [literally, 'He was everything'] belonging to Him in an immutable nature." Two fragments say that Jesus was "God put to death, the King of Israel slain." *On the Nature of Christ* states, "For, being at once both God and perfect man . . . as regards the flesh, He concealed the signs of His Deity, although He was the true God existing before all ages."

Two statements seem to indicate a preexistent Son distinct from the Father but identified as the Spirit. "The Father sen[t] His Son from heaven without a bodily form, that, when He should put on a body by means of the Virgin's womb, and be born man, He might save man" *(Discourse on Soul and Body)*. "He who was begotten before the light; He who is Creator together with the Father; He who is the Fashioner of man; He who is all in all . . . in the voice of the preacher, the Word; among spirits, the Spirit; in the Father, the Son; in God, God; King for ever and ever. . . . God who is from God; the Son who is from the Father; Jesus Christ the King for evermore" *(On Faith)*.

Theophilus

Theophilus became bishop of Antioch in 168 and died in 181, so he wrote near the end of this era. *To Autolycus* begins with a strong expression of God's oneness, giving a modalistic definition of titles that trinitarians later used to distinguish the persons of the Godhead. "The appearance of God is ineffable and indescribable, and cannot be seen by eyes of flesh. . . . For if I say He is Light, I name but His own work; if I call Him Mind, I speak but of His wisdom; if I say He is Spirit, I speak of

His breath; if I call Him Wisdom, I speak of His off-spring; if I call Him Strength, I speak of His sway; if I call Him Power, I am mentioning His activity; if Providence, I but mention His goodness; if I call Him Kingdom, I but mention His glory; if I call Him Lord, I mention His being judge; if I call Him Judge, I speak of Him as being just; if I call Him Father, I speak of all things as being from Him" (1:3). (The last clause appears in another edition as, "If Father, I say everything.") "Now we also confess that God exists, but that He is one, the creator, and maker, and fashioner of this universe; and we know that all things are arranged by His providence, but by Him alone" (3:9).

Theophilus held that the Word was originally inherent in God in an impersonal way but later became expressed or begotten, apparently becoming a distinct person. Theophilus seemed to identify the Word as the Spirit. "God, then, having His own Word internal within His own bowels, begat Him, emitting Him along with His own wisdom before all things. He had this Word as a helper in the things that were created by Him, and by Him He made all things. He is called 'governing principle,' because He rules, and is Lord of all things fashioned by Him. He, then, being Spirit of God, and governing principle, and wisdom, and power of the highest, came down upon the prophets, and through them spake of the creation of the world and of all other things. For the prophets were not when the world came into existence, but the wisdom of God which was in Him, and His holy Word which was always present with Him" (2:10).

The Word is the activity or revelation of the Father's person. "The God and Father, indeed, of all cannot be contained, and is not found in a place, for there is no place of His rest; but His Word, through whom He made all things, being His power and His wisdom, assuming the person of the Father and Lord of all, went to the garden in the person of God, and conversed with Adam. . . . But when God wished to make all that He determined on, He begot this Word, uttered, the first-born of all creation, not Himself being emptied of the Word (Reason), but having begotten Reason, and always conversing with His Reason. . . . [John 1:1 shows] us that at first God was alone, and the Word in Him. . . . The Word, then, being God, and being naturally produced from God, wherever the Father of the universe wills, He sends Him to any place; and He, coming, is both heard and seen, being sent by Him, and is found in a place" (2:22).

Two passages indicate an incipient trinitarianism. "The three days [of creation] which were before the luminaries, are types of the *Triados*, of God, and His Word, and His wisdom" (2:15). "But to no one less than to His own Word and wisdom did He say, 'Let Us make' (2:18). The former quotation uses the genitive case of the Greek word *trias*, which means "triad" and was later used for the trinity. The translators left it in the original Greek but capitalized it. Some say this is the first Christian use of the word *trinity*, but most scholars reserve that dubious distinction for Tertullian, who used the Latin word *trinitas* about 210. (See chapter 7.)

Tertullian clearly defined his term and used it to mean three persons or personalities—Father, Son, and Holy Spirit. By contrast, Theophilus mentioned his term only once in passing and did not define it. His meaning is unclear. From 2:15 and 2:18 it seems that his triad is

God, His Word, and His Wisdom. If these are three persons, then only the first person is truly God and eternal. The third person is not the Holy Spirit but Wisdom. To confuse matters further, Theophilus elsewhere identified Wisdom with the Word (2:10; 2:22) and the Holy Spirit with the Word (2:10). Moreover, he never said the triad was three persons but used the term *person* in a way incompatible with trinitarian doctrine, saying the Word, which is God's power and wisdom, assumed the person of the Father, the person of God (2:22). Theophilus's triad, then, seems to be a triad of revelation or activity, originally consisting of God and two supreme attributes of His. The second member of the triad later became distinct from God Himself in some way, but the third member is never clearly personalized or identified as the Holy Spirit.

Athenagoras

Athenagoras was a philosopher who reportedly lived in Athens. His *Plea for the Christians* (c. 177) reveals further development toward trinitarianism near the end of this age.

Athenagoras stated that God is one but taught a distinction between God and the Logos. "Our doctrine acknowledges one God, the Maker of this universe, who is Himself uncreated . . . but has made all things by the Logos which is from Him" (4).

He thought of God in a threefold revelation, or as a triad of some sort consisting of the Father, the Logos (Son, Wisdom), and the Spirit. "[Christians desire] this one thing alone, that they know God and His Logos, what is the oneness of the Son with the Father, what is the communion of the Father with the Son, what is the Spirit, what is the unity of these three, the Spirit, the Son, the Father, and their distinction in unity" (12). "We acknowledge a God, and a Son his Logos, and a Holy Spirit, united in essence,—the Father, the Son, the Spirit, because the Son is the Intelligence, Reason, Wisdom of the Father, and the Spirit an effluence, as light from fire" (24).

In this vague divine triad, the Logos and Holy Spirit emanated from the Father, who is identified as God. "He is God who has framed all things by the Logos, and holds them in being by His Spirit" (6). "The Son of God is the Logos of the Father, in idea and in operation . . . the Father and the Son being one. And, the Son being in the Father and the Father in the Son, in oneness and power of spirit, the understanding and reason of the Father is the Son of God. . . . He is the first product of the Father, not as having brought into existence (for from the beginning, God, who is the eternal mind, had the Logos in Himself, being from eternity instinct with Logos); but inasmuch as He came forth to be the idea and energizing power of all material things. . . . The Holy Spirit Himself also, which operates in the prophets, we assert to be an effluence of God, flowing from Him, and returning back again like a beam of the sun. . . . [We] speak of God the Father, and of God the Son, and of the Holy Spirit, and . . . declare both their power in union and their distinction in order" (10).

Conclusions

In the period from about 130 to 180, we find a progressive shifting away from the biblical doctrine of Oneness and the substantially identical views of the Post-Apostolic Age. The vague possible indications of a pre-existent Son by Pseudo-Barnabas and Hermas become explicit in the Age of the Greek Apologists.

Near the beginning of the age stood Aristides, whose doctrine of God was for the most part biblical Oneness, and the *Epistle to Diognetus*, which still retained a predominantly biblical view but began to separate God and the Word. At the apex of the age, Justin and his disciple Tatian clearly differentiated the Father and the Word as two distinct beings. By the end of the era, Theophilus and Athenagoras had begun to express a vague, undefined form of triadism, although the former still used some Oneness expressions. Melito still maintained a predominantly Oneness view of God, but even some of his terms had become distorted, at least as they have come down to us.

Justin, Tatian, Theophilus, and Athenagoras seized upon the popular concept of the Logos to gain acceptance for Christianity as the true and highest philosophy. They taught that the Logos was originally in God's mind, but for the purposes of creation and incarnation the Logos emerged from God (was begotten) as a distinct divine being, albeit dependent upon God and subordinate to Him. To them the Logos is the supreme agent of God. He was responsible for the divine appearances, anointings, and messages of God in the Old Testament. Since Greek thought said God was totally transcendent and impassible, only a lesser divine agent could interact with humanity, be moved by emotions, be incarnated as a man, and suffer on the behalf of humanity. These Apologists identified the Logos as the preexistent Son of God, who became Jesus Christ.

The following quotations summarize the Logos doctrine of the Apologists.

The Apologists did not have the biblical conception of the Logos, but one somewhat resembling that of Philo. To them the Logos, as He existed eternally in God, was simply the divine reason, without personal existence. With a view to the creation of the world, however, God generated the Logos out of His own being and thus gave Him personal existence. Essentially the Logos remains identical with God, but in view of His origin as a person He may be called a creature. Briefly stated, Christ is the divine reason, immanent in God, to which God gave a separate existence, and through which He reveals Himself. . . . It should be noted particularly that the Logos of the Apologists, in distinction from the philosophical Logos, had an independent personality.[1]

According to the Apologists, the Logos existed before he became incarnate. He existed as the divine reason (*nous*) in God, just as a thought exists in man before it issues forth in verbal utterance. To this preexistent Logos, Theophilus applied the word *endiathetos*, which was used by the Stoic philosophers and also by Plato. The Logos was conceived of as the divine immanent reason. . . . From all eternity the Father was Logos-natured. For the purpose of creation the Logos was projected as an independent personal being. By an exercise of God's will, the Logos sprang forth as the thought is uttered in speech. . . . The Logos was called "the first production of the Father," "the first-born work of the Father." . . . This personal differentiation of the Logos from God was something new, and it was

Christian when considered in the light of the Stoic philosophy. It should be noted, however, that according to the Apologists there was no personal differentiation of the Logos before the creation. Although Christ and the Logos were identified, the historical Christ was pushed into the background, and the Son of God was understood to be the pre-existent Logos.[2]

The Apologists affirmed that God is one, yet their Logos doctrine suggests ditheism (two gods) or binitarianism (two persons). The Apologists did not use the later trinitarian doctrines of coequality, coeternity, and consubstantiality to try to resolve this dilemma. Instead they adhered to an absolute monotheism before the begetting of the Logos and sought to maintain the monotheistic concept by presenting the Father as the supreme, true God and the Logos as subordinate in time, rank, power, and substance.

The Apologists said little about the Holy Spirit. Some passages indicate that the Holy Spirit is somehow distinct from the Father and the Logos, but they give no clear definition. The Apologists described the Logos as performing all the work that trinitarians later attributed to the Holy Spirit. Some passages seemingly identify the Holy Spirit with the Father, with the Logos, or as an impersonal force. When the Spirit is clearly differentiated from the Father and the Logos, He is a divine being of even lesser rank than the Logos, perhaps similar to an angel.

The Apologists' doctrine of God can be summarized as follows.

The Apologists taught the subordination of the Son to the Father. According to Justin, the Father alone is the real God; the Logos is only a Divine Being of second rank. . . . He is the Father's organ and servant, and is dependent on him. . . . The Apologists considered the Godhead a triad rather than a trinity. This is seen in the fact that while the Spirit was distinguished from the Logos and the Father, he was subordinated to both. Since the Logos inspired the prophets and was at work everywhere, there was little room for the activity of the Holy Spirit. Fortunately the Apologists had no occasion to speak to the heathen about the Holy Spirit, as they themselves had not clarified their ideas on the subject.[3]

The Apologists' doctrine was clearly not yet trinitarianism. It was an evolution away from the biblical doctrine of Oneness and toward later trinitarianism, not vice versa. Their view of God before the begetting of the Logos and their exegesis of John 1:1 were essentially Oneness. They deviated from the biblical doctrine by (1) equating the Son with the Logos (instead of defining the Son in terms of the Incarnation) and (2) interpreting the begetting of the Son as an act of God before creation whereby He made the Logos a distinct being. Their views were quite similar to those of Arius, whom the Council of Nicea condemned as a heretic in 325, although not as extreme.

Trinitarian scholars are forced to concede that the Greek Apologists were not orthodox trinitarians. They usually argue that we cannot judge the Apologists by the standards of a later age—that we cannot expect doctrinal precision before later controversies led to the formulation of orthodox terms, definitions, phrases, and creeds. This contention concedes that Scripture is not a sufficient standard and that the doctrine of the trinity has evolved over time. Although trinitarians would regard the Apologists' views as heretical today, they do not classify the Apologists as heretics, because the Apologists are their church fathers and their first theologians. If we cannot trust the views of the Apologists, however, why should we accept them as church fathers and adopt the doctrines of their theological descendants?

The Apologists probably did not represent the majority view of the Christian laity or pastors. Most of them, notably Justin, were not pastors or bishops. Their immersion in Greek philosophy heavily influenced their doctrine of God, but most early Christians were not philosophers and were not trained in classical Greek thought.

As an example, according to *The Martyrdom of Justin* (mid second century), a Christian named Hierax, who was executed with Justin, told the Roman prefect at his trial, "Christ is our true father, and faith in Him is our mother" (3). This statement seems to reflect the older view that Jesus is the one God, the Father, incarnate.

As chapters 9 and 10 will discuss, later evidence indicates that the majority of believers still adhered to the biblical doctrine of Oneness even in the early third century.

The
Old Catholic Age,
A.D. 170-325

6

Irenaeus

At the beginning of the Old Catholic Age stood Irenaeus (died c. 200). He was reared in Asia Minor but spent most of his life in the West and became bishop of Lyons in Gaul in 178. Historians typically speak of him as the first post-apostolic theologian because he enunciated a comprehensive doctrinal system based on the New Testament in opposition to heresies. The theology of Irenaeus is typically characterized as biblical, deeply reverential of tradition, and Christocentric.[1]

Older historians often described Irenaeus as a disciple of Polycarp, but it appears that Polyearp's influence on him was minimal. Evidently, as a young boy Irenaeus heard Polycarp preach and perhaps met him. Irenaeus wrote, "I also saw [Polycarp] in my early youth" (*Against Heresies* 3:3:4). Cyril Richardson explained, "He himself tells us that he had personal memories of the great Polycarp. . . . They seem more like the memories of a bright boy, vividly recalling the scenes of his childhood, than of a pupil of a theologian."[2]

Irenaeus used phrases and ideas from Justin, the foremost Greek Apologist. Thus he was probably "a pupil of Justin's as well as a reader of his books."[3] In contrast to

Justin and the other Greek Apologists, however, Irenaeus largely avoided philosophical speculation, particularly speculation about the Logos; instead he focused on the historical Christ as God incarnate and Savior.[4]

His major work was *Against Heresies*, which was particularly written against Gnosticism (c. 182-88). Although composed in Greek, it exists only in a Latin translation whose original text is often uncertain.[5]

One God in Threefold Revelation

Against Heresies teaches that God is one and speaks of Father, Son, and Holy Spirit. It says the universal faith of the church as delivered by the apostles is belief "in one God, the Father Almighty, Maker of heaven, and earth, and the sea, and all things that are in them; and in one Christ Jesus, the Son of God, who became incarnate for our salvation; and in the Holy Spirit, who proclaimed through the prophets the dispensations of God" (1:10:1).

Perhaps this statement displays a form of trinitarian thinking by its threefold emphasis and by its declaration that "the Son" became incarnate, which implies that the Son preexisted the Incarnation in a manner somehow distinct from the Father. On the other hand, the statement distinguishes Father, Son, and Holy Spirit in terms of manifestation or revelation rather than essence. Moreover, the same passage goes on to identify Jesus Christ as the visible manifestation of the invisible God and the One to whom every knee shall bow.

In a parallel statement, the language of manifestation is even more pronounced: "All receive one and the same God the Father, and believe in the same dispensation regarding the incarnation of the Son of God, and are cognizant of the same gift of the Spirit" (5:20: 1). Similarly, the Father is "the only and the true God," who grants, "by our Lord Jesus Christ, the governing power of the Holy Spirit" (3:6:4). The Word and the Spirit are "dispensations" of the Father (4:33:15).

All descriptions of the Deity "belong to one and the same name," to "one and the same Being" (2:35:3). The prophets announced one God "under various aspects . . . and many titles" (3:10:5). In one passage Irenaeus used four titles for God and then described God by a singular pronoun: "There is one God, the Father, and one Word, and one Son, and one Spirit, and one salvation to all who believe in Him" (4:6:7).

Irenaeus emphatically identified the Father as "the only God" (2:28:4) and as "the Creator" (4:1:2). "God the Creator . . . is the only God, the only Lord, the only Creator, the only Father, alone containing all things, and Himself commanding all things into existence" (2:1:1). (See also 2:30:9.) One Being is Father and God (4:1:1). He is the Creator (2:9:1), and our Creator is our Forgiver (5:17:3).

The Word/Son and Wisdom/Spirit

In contrast to the Greek Apologists, Irenaeus did not define the Logos as a second, subordinate person created by God at a point in time. Instead, the Logos is eternal, always in or with the Father. While some passages imply a distinction between the Father and the Logos, a number of passages describe the Logos as the mind of the Father or the revelation of the Father. "God over all . . . is all Nous [Mind], and all Logos [Word] . . . and has in Himself nothing more ancient or later than another, and nothing at variance with another, but continues altogether equal, and similar, and homogeneous" (2:13:8). "God is all mind, all reason, all active spirit, all light, and always exists one and the same" (2:28:4). "God being all Mind, and all Logos, both speaks exactly what He thinks, and thinks exactly what He speaks. For His thought is Logos, and Logos is Mind, and Mind comprehending all things is the Father Himself. He, therefore, who speaks of the mind of God, and ascribes to it a special origin of its own, declares Him a compound Being, as if God were one thing, and the original Mind another. . . . No man understands that production, or generation, or calling, or revelation, or by whatever name one may describe [the Word's] generation, which is in fact altogether indescribable. . . . The Father only . . . begat, and the Son . . . was begotten" (2:28:5).

The Word of God is "eternal" and is "God Himself" (2:13:8). The Word has always "been in the Father" (3:8:3) and has "co-existed" with Him (2:25:3). The Word of God is Jesus, who is God (3:9:3).

Irenaeus explained that God created by His Word, in the sense of thought, action, or utterance. "He created and made all things by His Word. . . . He Himself in Himself, after a fashion which we can neither describe nor conceive, predestinating all things, formed them as He pleased" (2:2:4). "His own Word is both suitable and sufficient for the formation of all things. . . . David also expresses the same truth, 'For He spake, and they were made; He commanded, and they were created'" (2:2:5). "As soon as God formed a conception in His mind, that was also done which He had thus mentally conceived. For it was not possible that one Being should mentally form the conception, and another actually produce the things which had been conceived by Him in His mind. . . . The Father had (ideally) formed [the world] in counsel with Himself" (2:3:2). "He is Father . . . who made those things by Himself, that is, through His Word and His Wisdom" (2:30:9).

The Word, who was the Creator, became flesh (3:11:4). The "Word of God the Father [became] the Son of man" (3:18:6).

Like Justin, however, Irenaeus used the term "Son of God" as the exact equivalent of "Word" instead of restricting it, as the Bible does, to the Incarnation. "The Word of God . . . became incarnate when the fulness of time had come, at which the Son of God had to become the Son of man" (3:16:7). (See also 3:16:3; 3:18:1-2).

Irenaeus spoke of the Holy Spirit as "the Spirit of the Father" (5:6:1). He identified God's Wisdom as the Spirit, unlike the Apologists (with the possible exception of Theophilus[6]), who followed Philo in equating Wisdom with the Word. "For with [God] were always present the Word and Wisdom, the Son and the Spirit, by whom and in whom, freely and spontaneously, He made all things, to whom also He speaks, saying, 'Let Us make man after Our image and likeness'" (4:20:1). "The Word, namely the Son, [was] always with the Father. . . . Wisdom also, which is the Spirit, was present with Him, anterior to all creation" (4:20:3). (See also 2:28:2.)

This terminology may imply personal distinctions in the Godhead. Some passages seem to reflect such a view—for example, the explanation that in Genesis 1:26 God spoke to Word and Wisdom (as Theophilus had said) or Son and Spirit (4:preface:4; 4:20:1). But if Word/Son and Wisdom/Spirit are additional divine persons then they are subordinate agents, "the Father planning everything well and giving His commands, the Son carrying these into execution and performing the work of creating, and the Spirit nourishing and increasing (what is made)" (4:38:3). Other passages seem to speak of them as manifestations, offices, or impersonal attributes. "In respect of His love, [God is] the Father; but in respect of His power, He is Lord; and in respect of His wisdom, our Maker and Fashioner" (5:17:1).

With respect to Genesis 1:26, Irenaeus elsewhere used an impersonal metaphor, saying the Father spoke to "the hands of God," by which He created Adam and also recreates us spiritually (5:1:3), and he spoke of the Father as creating in counsel with Himself (2:3:2). Morever, he described Word and Spirit as extensions or operations of the Father: "For the Father bears the creation and His own Word simultaneously, and the Word borne by the Father grants the Spirit to all as the Father wills. . . . The Father is indeed above all . . . but the Word is through all things . . . while the Spirit is in us all. . . . 'There is one Father, who is above all, and through all, and in us all'" (5:18:2).

The Deity of Jesus

Irenaeus identified Jesus Christ as God incarnate. "To Christ Jesus, our Lord, and God, and Saviour, and King, according to the will of the invisible Father, 'every knee should bow'" (1:10:1). "No other is named as God, or is called Lord, except Him who is God and Lord of all, who also said to Moses, 'I AM THAT I AM' . . . and His Son Jesus Christ our Lord" (3:6:2). No one is God or Lord except God the Father and His Word (3:15:3; 4:1:1). Jesus is God (3:9:3; 3:21:4). "Christ Himself, therefore, together with the Father, is the God of the living, who spake to Moses, and who was also manifested to the fathers" (4:5:2). Significantly, these passages say only the Father and Son are Lord and God, whereas a trinitarian expression would include the Holy Spirit also.

Moreover, Irenaeus spoke of Jesus as Father and Spirit. Citing Deuteronomy 32:6 he said, "The Word of God" is "our Father . . . the father of the human race" (4:31:2). And "He is indeed Saviour, as being the Son and Word of God; but salutary, since (He is) Spirit" (3:10:2). The Word created us, yet "all things were made" by "the Spirit of God," "the seed of the Father of all" (4:31:2).

In discussing the Word/Son, Irenaeus preserved the biblical concept of the Son as the revelation of the Father. "Through His Word, who is His Son, through Him [the Father] is revealed" (2:30:9). "The Lord [bore] witness, that in Himself they had both known and seen the Father" (3:13:2). "The Father therefore has revealed Himself to all, by making His Word visible to all" (4:6:5). "The Father is the invisible of the Son, but the Son the visible of the Father. And for this reason all spake with Christ when He was present (upon earth), and they named Him God" (4:6:6). The Father and Creator "'has visited us' through His Son" (5:17:1). Christ is the voice of God (5:17:2). "The Creator of the world is truly the Word of God: and this is our Lord, who in the last times was made man" (5:18:3).

Irenaeus interpreted certain Old Testament passages in a way that implies some sort of distinction between God and the Word before the Incarnation. The Word spoke to Adam in Genesis 3:8; Genesis 19:24 refers to the Father and the Son, the latter having spoken to Abraham; and Psalm 45:6 and 110:1 describe God speaking to the Word. (He adopted Justin's explanation for the latter three verses, yet in contrast to Justin he said the Father spoke to Moses in Exodus 3.) Moreover, "the Son, eternally co-existing with the Father, from of old, yea, from the beginning, always reveals the Father to Angels" (2:30:9). The Old Testament saints did not see the invisible Father in their visions but His Word, which showed the Father's brightness (4:20:11). Thus the Word/Son was God's communication, self-revelation, or visible manifestation even before the Incarnation.

If Irenaeus taught a distinction of persons, he considered it temporary, for he interpreted I Corinthians 15:24-28 to mean that in the end God's "offspring, the First-begotten Word . . . should be contained by Him; and . . . the creature [redeemed humans] should contain the Word, and ascend to Him" (5:36:1-2). Otto Heick interpreted Irenaeus to teach: "After all has been completed and the mission of Christ is accomplished, Christ's special position in the economy of the Trinity will cease. . . . There is a Trinity for the purpose of revelation only. After all has been accomplished, the distinction between the persons will cease."

The Name of God

Like the writers of the Post-Apostolic Age and unlike trinitarians such as Tertullian, Irenaeus retained a biblical doctrine of the name of God. He said the name of Jesus Christ belongs to and reveals the Father. Referring to Malachi 1:11, he said, "What other name is there which is glorified among the Gentiles than that of our Lord, by whom the Father is glorified, and man also? And because it is (the name) of His own Son, who was made man by Him, He calls it His own. . . . The Father confess[es] the name of Jesus Christ, which is throughout all the world glorified in the Church, to be His own. . . . Since,therefore, the name of the Son belongs to the Father, and since in the omnipotent God the Church makes offerings through Jesus Christ, He says well on both these grounds, 'And in every place incense is offered to My name, and a pure sacrifice'" (4:17:6).

The "Demonstration"

The last major work of Irenaeus was the *Demonstration of the Apostolic Preaching*, which has come to us in only one manuscript (1265-89) of an Armenian translation (c. 600) that has many probable but unidentifiable corruptions.[8] It too speaks of the Father, Son/Word, and Spirit/Wisdom, using the language of attributes or manifestations. "God is rational, and therefore produced creatures by His Word, and God is a spirit, and so fashioned everything by His Spirit. . . . The Word is fitly and properly called the Son, but the Spirit the Wisdom of God" (5). There are three articles of faith: "God the Father"; "the Word of God, the Son of God Christ Jesus our Lord"; and "the Holy Spirit" (6). "The Son, according to the Father's good-pleasure, administers the Spirit charismatically as the Father wills" (7).

Irenaeus apparently used a threefold baptismal formula linked to his understanding of God. "We have received baptism for remission of sins in the name of God the Father, and in the name of Jesus Christ, the Son of God, who became incarnate and died and was raised, and in the Holy Spirit of God" (3). "The baptism of our rebirth comes through these three articles, granting us rebirth unto God the Father, through His Son, by the Holy Spirit. For those who are bearers of the Spirit of God are led to the Word, that is, to the Son; but the Son takes them and presents them to the Father; and the Father confers incorruptibility" (7).

Like Justin but unlike trinitarians today, Irenaeus retained the name of Jesus in his baptismal formula, apparently in deference to the original practice and as part of his concept that the name of Jesus belongs to the Father. Interestingly, in his earlier writing, he cited Acts 2:38 and 4:12 to teach that believers are baptized into Jesus Christ for the remission of sins *(Against Heresies* 3:12:2, 4, 7). And a fragment from his lost writings indicates that he regarded the name of Jesus as vital in baptism: "We are made clean, by means of the sacred water and the invocation of the Lord" *(Fragments* 34). Perhaps Irenaeus referred to his threefold formula that included the name of Jesus, perhaps he originally baptized in Jesus' name but later changed formulas, or perhaps the Armenian manuscript was distorted by later trinitarians.

In any case, it is amazing that many Protestants cite Irenaeus as an authority for a trinitarian baptismal formula but reject his clear teaching that baptism is part of the new birth and effective for the remission of sins. (They typically say that such a view is legalistic, heretical, or even cultic.)

Conclusions

Irenaeus retained much of the emphasis, terminology, and concepts of the Bible and of the Post-Apostolic Age.

Many of his statements sound like modern Oneness. Namely, he emphasized that there is only one God, identified the one God as the Father, described the Word as the mind and expression of the Father, described the Son as the visible revelation of the invisible Father, taught that Jesus is God, and identified the name of Jesus as belonging to the Father. In these respects, his doctrine resembles what the modalists emphasized in contrast to their trinitarian opposition (although these points can also be interpreted as compatible with modern trinitarianism). And unlike major writers immediately after him, he never attacked the modalists. To the extent that his theology differs from Oneness, it appears to introduce variations on an earlier Oneness theme.

The influence of Justin seems to account for most of Irenaeus's apparent deviations from Oneness. While Irenaeus did not fully adopt the Logos doctrine of the Greek Apologists, his terminology and ideas were somewhat affected by them. Consequently, unlike modalism and unlike modern Oneness, he equated "Son of God" with "Word" and "Holy Spirit" with "Wisdom," and he apparently used a threefold baptismal formula, at least in his later years.

It is not altogether clear whether Irenaeus regarded the Son/Word and Spirit/Wisdom primarily as impersonal aspects of God's nature, as first impersonal and then personal in some sense, or as eternally distinct from the Father. It seems that he thought of an impersonal Word eternally in the Father that, for the purpose of God's self-revelation, became somehow distinct from the Father, although in an incomprehensible way and not as the Apologists taught. He did not clearly distinguish the Holy

Spirit as a person. Perhaps he was inconsistent on these points, modified his views over time, or sought a compromise formulation. Perhaps key statements were deleted, garbled, or inserted in the transmission process.

Irenaeus taught a threefold revelation of God. Although at times he interpreted scriptural passages in a way that could indicate personal distinctions, he was not consistent or definitive as to the nature of those distinctions. He apparently associated the threeness with dispensations, operations, or activities of God, not with God's essence. At most, then, trinitarians could argue that he believed in an economic trinity, which means making trinitarian distinctions with respect to God's activity or operations in the world (rather than with respect to God's essence). But if he believed in three persons in the Godhead, then for him the Father is the supreme Deity, and the Son and Spirit are derivative divine agents.

Consequently, trinitarian historians have correctly rendered the following verdict: "Irenaeus made but a small contribution to a successfully articulated dogma of the Trinity. This was chiefly due to his refusal to deal with speculative questions."[9] "Irenaeus goes no further than the baptismal formula and the trinity of revelation. . . . Of a supramundane trinity of essence he betrays but faint indication."[10]

7

Early Trinitarians: Tertullian, Origen, and Others

In the beginning of the third century we find the first clearly identifiable trinitarian language. The person most responsible for the development of trinitarianism in its earliest stage was Tertullian, the first major theologian to write in Latin. The second most influential person was Origen, who championed trinitarianism in the East as Tertullian did in the West. Following them were a number of writers who were trinitarian of one sort or another. This chapter analyzes the doctrine of God expressed by these earliest confessed trinitarians.

Tertullian

Tertullian (c. 150-225) was a lawyer and rhetorician who converted in middle age (c. 195) and became a local church presbyter in Carthage, North Africa. He is commonly called the founder of Western theology.[1] He was the first writer to speak of God as a trinity and as three persons in one substance.[2]

About 207, Tertullian joined the Montanists, a schismatic group that had been expelled from the institutional church, and thereafter he attacked the church vehemently. *Against Praxeas*, his famous attack on modalism and definitive presentation of trinitarianism, was written well after that time; scholars today conclude that it was probably written in 213.

Apparently, Tertullian started with a binitarian (two-person) concept much like that of the Greek Apologists. In an early work, *On Prayer*, he identified Jesus Christ as the "Spirit of Word" and "Spirit of God" (1). Even in *Against Praxeas* he identified the Holy Spirit in Luke 1:35 as the Word (26). Although that work names the Spirit a third person, it devotes little attention to the subject.

The Montanists emphasized the work of the Spirit. Although Hippolytus and others said that some of them were modalists (perhaps all of them initially), Jaroslav Pelikan has speculated that their emphasis on the Holy Spirit may have influenced Tertullian's doctrine of the trinity. He suggested:

> Montanism taught Tertullian to think of the Paraclete in more personal terms than he had in his early works, so that he came to a more metaphysical doctrine of the Trinity. . . . The great influence of Tertullian on the subsequent trinitarian discussion would mean, then, that while some Montanists held to a naive formula for the Trinity that was shared by other Christians, Tertullian's Montanism helped him to insights by which the church eventually transcended this formula and developed a more consistent doctrine of the Trinity.[3]

At the same time, Pelikan acknowledged that Tertullian probably changed Montanism as much as he was changed by it, noting that he lived two generations after its founding.[4]

According to Tertullian's book *Against Hermogenes*, originally God existed alone. He was not yet the Father because the Son did not yet exist (3). The Son, also called Word and Wisdom, was "born and created" by the Father, who is therefore older, nobler, stronger, and more powerful than he (18).

Tertullian stated his trinitarian doctrine most clearly in *Against Praxeas*. God is the "Trinity," which consists of "three Persons" —Father, Son, and Holy Ghost (2). God is "one only substance in three coherent and inseparable (Persons)" (12). Thus three "beings" are God, but there is only one God (13).

In particular, the Father and the Son are "two separate Persons" (4), "two different Beings" (4), and "distinct but not separate" (11). The Son is "another" from the Father "on the ground of Personality, not of Substance—in the way of distinction, not of division" (12).

Although Tertullian spoke of one substance, his analogies reveal that the Son is subordinate to the Father and the Spirit is subordinate to both, for he compared the trinity to root, tree, fruit; sun, ray, apex of ray; and fountain, river, stream. "The Trinity, flowing down from the Father, does not at all disturb the Monarchy [one sovereign God], whilst it at the same time guards the state of the Economy [three persons]" (8). The Son and Spirit "have the second and the third places assigned to them" (3).

Both Father and Son can be called God, but when invoked together, the former is called God and the latter is called Lord. As an analogy, "I should give the name of 'sun' even to a sunbeam, considered in itself; but if I were mentioning the sun from which the ray emanates, I certainly should at once withdraw the name of sun from the mere beam. For although I make not two suns, still I shall reckon both the sun and its ray to be as much two things and two forms of one undivided substance, as God and His Word, as the Father and the Son" (13). "The Father is the entire substance, but the Son is a derivation and portion of the whole. . . . The Father is . . . greater than the Son" (9). The Son is merely "a portion of the whole Godhead" (26).

In response to the modalists, who said his doctrine divided God's one substance, Tertullian taught that even the angels "are naturally members of the Father's own substance"; if their existence does not destroy God's oneness, then neither should the existence of the Son and Spirit (3). This reasoning makes the Son and Spirit inferior to the Father, and it leads to tritheism.

Like the Greek Apologists before him, Tertullian said that originally the Word was impersonally inherent in God but became a distinct person at a point in time, when he was begotten. "Before all things God was alone. . . . Yet even not then was He alone; for He had with Him that which He possessed in Himself, that is to say, His own Reason. . . . God had not Word from the beginning, but He had Reason even before the beginning. . . . For although God had not yet sent out His Word, He still had Him within Himself" (5). He identified the begetting with Genesis 1:3. "The Word also Himself assume[d] His own form and glorious garb, His own sound and vocal utterance, when God says, 'Let there be light.' This is the perfect nativity of the Word,

when He proceeds forth from God—formed by Him first
. . . then afterward begotten" (7).

Clearly, to Tertullian the trinitarian distinctions had a
beginning. He also believed that they would have an ending, as shown by his comment on I Corinthians 15:24-25:
"The Monarchy. . . remains so firm and stable in its own
state, notwithstanding the introduction into it of the
Trinity, that the Son actually has to restore it entire to the
Father" (4).

In answering objections, Tertullian explained that
Isaiah 44:6 means God has no God beside Himself with
reference to idolatry; namely, God meant, "Beside me
there is none else, except my Son" (18). Similarly, Isaiah
44:24 means He stretched out the heaven "alone with His
Son" or "the Son stretched out the heaven alone, because
He alone ministered in the Father's work" (19).

Following a concept in Stoicism, Tertullian believed
that every spirit has a bodily substance, and he apparently thought each member of the trinity has a distinct
body—a very tritheistic concept. "For who will deny that
God is a body, although 'God is a Spirit?' For Spirit has a
bodily substance of its own kind, in its own form. . . .
Whatever, therefore, was the substance of the Word that I
designate a Person, I claim for it the name of Son" (7).

Tertullian taught triple immersion in a trinitarian baptismal formula, becoming the first theologian to use Matthew 28:19 as a precise baptismal formula and as a proof
text for trinitarianism. We are "to baptize into the Father
and the Son and the Holy Ghost, not into a unipersonal
God. And indeed it is not once only, but three times, that
we are immersed into the Three Persons, at each several
mention of Their names" (26).

Clement and Origen

Clement of Alexandria (died before 216) and his pupil Origen (c. 185-254) were local church presbyters in Alexandria and teachers there in a theological school for converts. Pantaenus, a converted Stoic philosopher, is the first known superintendent of this school. He was followed in that position by Clement and then Origen.

More than merely principals of a local institute, Clement and Origen are considered to be the leaders of the Alexandrian school of theology. As Heick explained, "The Alexandrian School was a continuation of the principles which were expressed by Philo and by the Greek Apologists. This school marked the first consistent synthesis between biblical revelation and philosophical speculation."[5] It was characterized by an emphasis on knowledge as greater than faith, by an extremely allegorical interpretation of Scripture, and by its focus on the Logos. This theological system is often described as Christian Gnosticism.

Clement, a pagan philosopher before his conversion, was the chief founder of the Alexandrian system of theology, and he incorporated many pagan ideas into his beliefs. His doctrine of God seems close to that of the Greek Apologists. He spoke of the Word and Spirit but did not clearly express personal distinctions.

Originally the Word "was in God"; the Word created us and later manifested himself as Christ (*Exhortations to the Heathen*, 1). *The Instructor* seemingly identifies the Word with the Spirit, calling Jesus the "Spirit and Word. . . . the Word of God, the Spirit made flesh" (1:6). Later, however, it contains a prayer that thanks "the Alone Father and Son, Son and

Father, the Son, Instructor and Teacher, with the Holy Spirit all in One" (3:12).

Miscellanies briefly mentions that Plato wrote about the "Holy Trinity" or triad, namely, the Father, Son, and Holy Spirit (5:14). It also calls the Son "the timeless and unoriginated First Principle, and Beginning of existences . . . from whom we are to learn the remoter Cause, the Father, of the universe, the most ancient and the most beneficient of all" (7:1). It identifies the Son as the Father's Word and His Wisdom (7:2).

Fragments from Cassiodorus speak of the eternal generation of the Son (3), but Cassiodorus, the sixth-century compiler, admitted that he corrected Clement freely.

Origen was the most influential representative of the Alexandrian school. He was the first and foremost champion of trinitarianism in the East, as Tertullian was in the West, and he wrote against modalism. Pelikan identified him as the primary developer of the trinitarian Logos/Son doctrine, with Tertullian and Novatian being next in importance.[6]

Origen taught a number of strange doctrines derived from speculation and Greek philosophy, such as the pre-existence of souls, universalism, the ultimate salvation of Satan, and eternal creation. Although he typically interpreted Scripture very allegorically, he took Matthew 19:12 to the extreme of literalism and castrated himself. Because of his heretical doctrines, Origen was excommunicated by a synod presided over by Bishop Demetrius in 231, and he was formally anathematized by councils in 543 and 553, but he still remained popular in many segments of the institutional church.

According to his most comprehensive work, *On the Principles*, the apostles taught that "there is one God," that Jesus "was born of the Father before all creatures," and that "the Holy Spirit was associated in honour and dignity with the Father and the Son. But in His case it is not clearly distinguished whether He is to be regarded as born or innate, or also as a Son of God or not" (preface:4).

Origen was the first writer to teach clearly the doctrine of an eternal trinity of persons. He taught that the Son was eternal (1:2:2), that the Son was eternally being generated by the Father (1:2:4), and that the Holy Spirit was eternal (1:3:4; 4:1:28). He also practiced trinitarian baptism (1:3:2).

In some passages, Origen approached the doctrine of coequality, saying that "nothing in the Trinity can be called greater or less" (1:3:7). Yet he also said that the Son was "created" by the Father (1:2:1) and subject to Him (3:5:6-7). He spoke of the Father as the source and the Son as the image (1:2:5-6).

In his *Commentary on John* Origen subordinated the Son to the Father and the Spirit to the Son, and he used tritheistic language. "God the Word is a separate being and has an essence of His own" (1:23). The Father alone is "the God" (*ho theos*); the Son is simply "God" without the article (*theos*), that is, God in a secondary or relative sense. "God on the one hand is Very God (Autotheos, God of Himself) . . . but . . . all beyond the Very God is made God by participation in His divinity, and is not to be called simply God (with the article), but rather God (without the article). And thus the first-born of all creation, who is the first to be with God, and to attract to Himself divinity, is a being of more exalted rank than the other gods beside Him, of whom God is the God" (2:2).

"The Father [is] the one true God, but . . . other beings besides the true God . . . have become gods by having a share of God. . . . The Father is the fountain of divinity, the Son of reason. . . . There was God with the article and God without the article, then there were gods in two orders, at the summit of the higher order of whom is God the Word, transcended Himself by the God of the universe. And, again, there was the Logos with the article and the Logos without the article, corresponding to God absolutely and a god; and the Logos in two ranks" (2:3).

"We consider, therefore, that there are three hypostases [persons], the Father and the Son and the Holy Spirit; and at the same time we believe nothing to be uncreated but the Father. . . . The Holy Spirit is the most excellent and the first in order of all that was made by the Father through Christ. . . . The Holy Spirit seems to have need of the Son, to minister to Him His essence, so as to enable Him not only to exist, but to be wise and reasonable and just" (2:6).

In *Against Celsus*, Origen called the Son "the most ancient of all the works of creation" (5:37) and a "second God" (5:39). Moreover, the Son is "inferior" to the Father (8:15).

Origen was concerned because many Christian prayed directly to Jesus Christ; therefore, in *On Prayer* he taught that they should not address the Son directly in prayer but "the Father through the Son in the Holy Spirit" (100:15).[7]

Hippolytus

Hippolytus (died c. 236) was a pupil of Irenaeus, but his doctrine of God resembles that of Tertullian rather than Irenaeus. He vehemently opposed the modalist teacher Noetus, and he attacked the Roman bishops Zephyrinus and Callistus, accusing them of embracing modalism and bitterly impugning their character. He was excommunicated by Callistus and headed a small rival church in the Rome area; in Roman Catholic terms he was the first antipope.

In *Against the Heresy of One Noetus* Hippolytus taught a trinity (*triados*) of one God in three persons (14), the Son and Spirit being subordinate to the Father. He used the analogies of water from a fountain and a ray from the sun to describe the Son and Father, saying, "There is but one power, which is from the All; and the Father is the All, from whom cometh this Power, the Word" (11). Moreover, "it is the Father who commands, and the Son who obeys, and the Holy Spirit who gives understanding" (14).

Curiously for a trinitarian, he acknowledged some distinction in terms between "Word" and "Son": "Neither was the Word, prior to incarnation and when by Himself, yet perfect Son, although He was perfect Word, only-begotten" (15). Perhaps his discussions with the modalists forced him to this position, for they maintained that the title of Son related to the Incarnation.

In *The Refutation of all Heresies*, Hippolytus taught that the Logos was begotten at a certain time. "The first and only (one God), both Creator and Lord of all, had nothing coeval with Himself. . . . But He was One, alone in Himself" (10:28). "This solitary and supreme Deity, by an exercise of reflection, brought forth the Logos first . . . conceived and residing in the divine mind" (10:29). The Logos then became the agent of creation (10:29).

Novatian

Novatian (died c. 257) of Rome was a vigorous trinitarian opponent of Sabellius and an influential architect of trinitarianism. He was later excommunicated by Cornelius, bishop of Rome, for teaching that forgiveness was not available for certain sins committed after baptism. He headed a large schismatic group; in Roman Catholic terms he was the second antipope.

His *Treatise Concerning the Trinity* affirms the divinity of Jesus and teaches that the Word is a second subordinate person begotten at a point in time. "God the Father, the founder and creator of all things, who only knows no beginning, invisible, infinite, immortal, eternal, is one God . . . of whom, when He willed it the Son, the Word, was born. . . . He then, since He was begotten of the Father, is always in the Father. And I thus say always, that I may show Him not to be unborn, but born" (31). The Word is "inferior to the Father" (27).

Cyprian

Cyprian (died 258) was a disciple of Tertullian who became bishop of Carthage in North Africa two years after his baptism and served in that capacity for ten years until his martyrdom. He taught some form of trinitarianism, saying "the three are one" ("To Jubaianus," *Epistles* 72:12). In opposition to Stephen, bishop of Rome, he maintained that any baptism performed by "heretics" (groups not in fellowship with the organized church) was invalid. Some of them practiced trinitarian baptism (74:9, 11). Others baptized in the name of Jesus Christ, but Cyprian opposed their practice as contrary to trinitarianism. He argued that the Jews properly received baptism "in the name of Jesus Christ" as Peter instructed in Acts 2:38 only because they already acknowledged the Father (72:17), but Gentiles who did not acknowledge the Father must be baptized "in the full and united Trinity" according to Matthew 28:19 (72:18). He accused the "heretics" of not properly honoring "the name of the Father" (72:19), but he did not seem to be equally concerned about the name of the Holy Spirit.

Preserved in Cyprian's epistles is a letter from Cornelius, bishop of Rome, about people who rejoined his church and confessed "one God . . . one Christ the Lord . . . and one Holy Spirit" (45:2).

Other Writers of the Age

Dionysius, bishop of Rome, opposed both modalism and tritheism. In *Against the Sabellians* (259-69) he said that some opponents of Sabellius, "by dividing and rending the monarchy, which is the most august announcement of the Church of God, into as it were, three powers, and distinct substances (hypostases), and three deities, destroy it. . . . These in a certain manner announce three gods, in that they divide the holy unity into three different substances, absolutely separated from one another" (1). Interestingly, he objected to the same term later used by orthodox trinitarians to mean "person": the Greek word *hupostasis*.

Dionysius (200-65), bishop of Alexandria and a pupil

of Origen, wrote against Sabellius in tritheistic and sub-ordinationistic terms, saying, "The Son of God is a creature and something made, not his own by nature, but alien in essence from the Father. . . . Being a creature, he did not exist before he came into being."[8] According to Athanasius, under criticism from Dionysius of Rome he later modified or clarified his more extreme statements. His *Epistle to Dionysius of Rome* as quoted by Athanasius affirms that the Son is eternal (1:4), eternally begotten (1:3), and of the same substance with God (6).

Gregory Thaumaturgus (died c. 270) was a converted philosopher and a pupil of Origen. He possibly taught the coequality of Father, Son, and Spirit. Gregory of Nyssa and Basil cited him as an ante-Nicene champion of the Nicene doctrine and attributed great miracles to him, but Eusebius did not mention either his trinitarian doctrine or his miracles. His *Declaration of Faith* was supposedly revealed to him in a vision by the apostle John at the request of Mary the mother of Jesus. It affirms a coequal, coeternal trinity, but Philip Schaff and other historians concluded that the statements about coequality and coeternity were added or expanded by a later copyist.[9]

Arnobius (c. 300), a North African, wrote in *Against the Heathen* that Jesus is to be worshiped (37) and regarded as God (39). "He is God in reality and without any shadow of doubt" (42). "He was God on high, God in His inmost nature . . . and was sent by the Ruler of all as a Saviour God" (53).

Lactantius (260-330), a prolific Latin writer with an excellent writing style, spoke of two persons in the God-head, making no mention of the Holy Spirit as a third person. "When we say that we worship one God only, we nevertheless assert that there are two, God the Father and God the Son . . . two persons" (*The Divine Institutes* 4:29). The Son was "twice born" (4:13) and is subordinate to the Father in time and essence. "There is one God alone, free, most high, without any origin; for He Himself is the origin of all things, and in Him at once both the Son and all things are contained. . . . Whatever is in the Father flows on to the Son, and whatever is in the Son descends from the Father" (4:29).

There were other writers of the time whom we will not discuss because they did not address the doctrine of God sufficiently or because only fragments of their works remain. They include Minucius Felix, who wrote much apologetic material with little doctrinal content; Julius Africanus; Methodius; Lucian, who was accused of advocating a form of Arianism and whom Arius spoke of as his teacher; Victorinus; and various minor writers.

Conclusions

Tertullian was the first person to teach explicitly the doctrine of one God in three persons. He invented many concepts and terms later used to define trinitarian orthodoxy. In the words of Louis Berkhof, he "enlarged the doctrine of the Logos into a doctrine of the Trinity" and "was the first to assert clearly the tri-personality of God, and to maintain the substantial unity of the three Persons."[10]

Ironically, the founder of trinitarianism was heretical by orthodox trinitarian standards, for he denied the doctrines of coeternity and coequality, subordinating the Son and Spirit to the Father as to time, power, and rank.

Origen advanced the doctrine of the trinity considerably by introducing the doctrine of the eternal generation of the Son.[11] Unlike Tertullian, he affirmed the doctrine of coeternity, but like Tertullian, he still retained a definite subordination of Son and Spirit to the Father and used tritheistic language. In the later Athanasian-Arian controversy that culminated at the Council of Nicea in 325, both sides appealed to Origen's writings, the Athanasians citing his doctrine of eternal generation, which implied an equality of substance in the Father and the Son, and the Arians citing his doctrine of subordination, which implied a difference of substance.

Most of the major writings that have survived from the time of Tertullian and Origen onward express trinitarian concepts. Hippolytus, Novatian, Cyprian, Dionysius of Rome, Dionysius of Alexandria, and Gregory Thaumaturgus were all trinitarians of sorts. Like Tertullian and Origen, most of them used quite tritheistic language on occasion and held to a doctrine of subordination. Their main emphasis was the distinction between the Father and Son and the subordination of the latter to the former. Thus, like the Greek Apologists, the earliest trinitarians did not accept the absolute deity of Jesus Christ, not even to the extent that later trinitarians would.

The doctrine of the Holy Spirit was still largely unexplored. More than most, Novatian emphasized the Holy Spirit as a third person. On the other hand, Arnobius and Lactantius ignored or rejected the idea that the Holy Spirit is a third person.

Of all the writers of this age, only Dionysius of Rome and possibly Gregory Thaumaturgus seemed to define trinitarianism in a way compatible with later Nicene orthodoxy.

The developing trinitarianism of these writers did not go unopposed. As chapters 8, 9, and 10 will discuss, it appears that a number of teachers and writers advocated Oneness concepts during the Old Catholic Age.

8

Baptism in the Name of Jesus

Most church historians agree that the original Christian baptismal formula was "in the name of Jesus" (typically with the title of Lord or Christ).[1] In the Post-Apostolic Age, Hermas and probably Clement of Rome alluded to baptism in Jesus' name, and one passage in the *Didache* refers to this formula. The emphasis on the name of Jesus by both Clement and Ignatius further indicates that the church of this age practiced baptism in Jesus' name.

The Age of the Greek Apologists provides the first definite evidence for a threefold formula. Even so, those who used such a formula, such as Justin and later Irenaeus, continued to include the name of Jesus. When Marcion's followers broke away from the church near the beginning of that age they continued to follow the formula that the church was using, which was "in the name of Jesus Christ." The early Montanists, who split off at the beginning of the Old Catholic Age, also apparently used the Jesus Name formula. (See chapter 9.)

The earliest evidence for the modern trinitarian formula is provided by one passage of the *Didache* (probably interpolated), by Tertullian, and by Origen. This formula is apparently the product of the Old Catholic Age. Nevertheless, the evidence discussed in this chapter shows that baptism in the name of Jesus was still widespread during this time.

Evidence in Popular Literature

The popular literature of the age provides evidence for baptism in Jesus' name. Various apocryphal, anonymous, and pseudonymous books give us a glimpse of prevalent practices among the common people. These writings are not always reliable doctrinally, but they preserve evidence of typical baptismal practices. Since they were not written by well-known church leaders, teachers, or "heretics" and since they were not used primarily for doctrinal authority, it seems that later scribes were not as concerned about insuring their doctrinal purity. Thus, works of this kind were less subject to alteration or destruction for doctrinal reasons.

Acts of Paul and Thecla (a second-century work probably by an Asiatic presbyter): "In the name of Jesus Christ I am baptized on my last day."

Acts of Peter and Paul: "We positively believe in our Lord Jesus Christ, into whom we have been baptized."

Recognitions of Clement (part of the Pseudo-Clementine literature of the late second or early third century): "[Jesus] instituted baptism by water amongst them, in which they might be absolved from all their sins on the invocation of His name. . . . Every one who, believing in this Prophet who had been foretold by Moses, is baptized in His name" (1:39).

The *Gospel of Philip* also speaks of baptism in the name of Jesus (2:3:72).[2]

Evidence Preserved by Cyprian

Cyprian wrote of many "heretics" in his day who baptized in the name of Jesus. The evidence surrounding this controversy indicates that many people in the institutional church also baptized in Jesus' name. Cyprian did not object to people in the church who baptized in Jesus' name, but he opposed accepting the baptism of "heretics" simply on the basis that they had invoked the name of Jesus.

Those who disagreed with him felt that the name of Jesus was so powerful in baptism that it was efficacious even for schismatics. Their position shows how highly people regarded baptism in Jesus' name even during this time of change and compromise. Both sides agreed that baptism was necessary for remission of sins and salvation, and everyone agreed that baptism in Jesus' name within the mainstream church was valid.

In opposition to Stephen, bishop of Rome, Cyprian maintained that any baptism performed by heretics was invalid. In a letter to Jubaianus in 256, be opposed the teaching that "all who are baptized everywhere, and in any manner, in the name of Jesus Christ, have obtained the grace of baptism" *(Epistles* 72:16). He asked, "Can they who among the heretics are said to be baptized in the name of Christ be judged to have obtained remission of sins?" and answered no (72:17).

Cyprian conceded that Peter taught baptism in Jesus' name in Acts 2:38 but argued that this baptism was for the Jews, since they already acknowledged the Father (72:17). Gentiles who did not already acknowledge the Father should not be baptized "in the name of Jesus Christ" but must be baptized in the trinity (72:18). Cyprian accused the heretics of not properly honoring the name of the Father in their baptism (72:19). Presumably, he did not object to someone being baptized into the church in Jesus' name if he already honored the Father properly as the believers in Acts did.

Among Cyprian's correspondence is a letter written in 256 by Firmilian, bishop of Caesarea in Cappadocia, against Stephen. It quotes Stephen as teaching: "The name of Christ is of great advantage to faith and the sanctification of baptism; so that whosoever is anywhere soever baptized in the name of Christ, immediately obtains the grace of Christ" (74:18).

Cyprian wrote against Stephen to Pompey, arguing that if the church denied that heretics received the Holy Spirit in the name of Jesus it should also deny that they received valid water baptism in the name of Jesus. "If they attribute the effect of baptism to the majesty of the name, so that they who are baptized anywhere and anyhow, in the name of Jesus Christ, are judged to be renewed and sanctified; wherefore, in the name of the same Christ, are not hands laid upon the baptized persons among them, for the reception of the Holy Spirit?" (73:5).

"A Treatise on Rebaptism"

A Treatise on Rebaptism by an anonymous writer, probably a third-century bishop who opposed Cyprian, demonstrates that many people both inside and outside the institutional church baptized in the name of Jesus. The treatise discusses what should be done about persons "who, although baptized in heresy, have yet been baptized in the name of our Lord Jesus Christ" and who turn from their heresy to the church (1). It concludes that rebaptism is not necessary: "Heretics who are already baptized in water in the name of Jesus Christ must only be baptized with the Holy Spirit" (12).

The treatise makes a number of significant points. First, its position had overwhelming support: the support of "the most ancient custom and ecclesiastical tradition" (1), "the venerable authority of all the churches" (2), "the authority of so many years, and so many churches and apostles and bishops" (6), and "the custom and authority which so much claim our veneration for so long a time and for such great men" (15). These phrases indicate not only the acceptance of baptism performed outside the institutional church but strong support specifically for baptism in the name of Jesus.

Second, the name of Jesus is significant and effective in baptism. Acts 4:12 and Philippians 2:9-11 show that "the power of the name of Jesus invoked upon any man by baptism . . . afford[s] to him . . . no slight advantage for the attainment of salvation" (6). The invocation of Jesus' name alone does not bring salvation to the heretic, but if he corrects his error, acknowledges the truth, and receives the Holy Spirit, then it becomes effective; the heretic does not "lose that former invocation of the name of Jesus" (6). In fact, the one baptism of Ephesians 4:5 is baptism in the name of Jesus. "When the apostle said that there was 'one baptism,' it must needs have been by the continued effect of the invocation of the name of Jesus, because, once invoked, it cannot be taken away by man" (10).

The treatise argues that baptism in Jesus' name does not contradict Matthew 28:19. "Neither must you esteem what our Lord said as being contrary to this treatment:

'Go ye, teach the nations; baptize them in the name of the Father, and of the Son, and of the Holy Ghost.' Because, although this is true and right, and to be observed by all means in the Church, and moreover has been used to be observed, yet it behoves us to consider that invocation of the name of Jesus ought not to be thought futile by us on account of the veneration and power of that very name, in which name all kinds of power are accustomed to be exercised, and occasionally some even by men outside the Church. . . . Therefore ought this invocation of the name of Jesus to be received as a certain beginning of the mystery of the Lord common to us and to all others, which may afterwards be filled up with the remaining things" (7).

Either the author thought that both a threefold formula and the Jesus Name formula were acceptable, or else he concluded that invoking Jesus' name was the proper fulfillment of Matthew 28:19. The latter conclusion is supported by his statements that "the invocation of the name of Jesus" in baptism fulfills the "one baptism" of Ephesians 4:5 and that it is something "common to us and to all others."

This document also reports that not only were heretics baptized by "invoking the name of the Lord Jesus," but many people, both "Jews and Gentiles, fully believing as they ought, are in like manner baptized" (12).

Other References

Apostolic Constitutions (or *Constitutions of the Holy Apostles*) was written in the fourth century or later, but it contains elements from earlier times. It speaks of "every lay Christian, upon whom the name of our Lord Jesus Christ is called" (8:44).

Appended to it are the Canons of Hippolytus; in the collection of Dionysius, canon 50, which is of late origin, reveals that there was a controversy over trinitarian baptism and insists upon three immersions in the three titles. "If any bishop or presbyter does not perform the three immersions of the one admission, but one immersion, which is given into the death of Christ, let him be deprived. . . . Do ye, therefore, O bishops, baptize thrice into one Father, and Son, and Holy Ghost." It seems that some bishops and presbyters were refusing to use the trinitarian formula even in the fourth century.

At this point, the collection of John of Damascus adds a condemnation of modalism and of the idea "that there is one God with three names." Apparently, the condemned baptism was single immersion in the name of Jesus Christ, which was viewed as an endorsement of a modalistic concept of God. Here, then, is evidence that the baptismal formula was associated with controversies over the Godhead. It seems that those who denied trinitarianism but upheld the deity of Jesus refused to use the trinitarian formula but baptized in Jesus' name.

Conclusions

Baptism in the name of Jesus was the practice of the apostolic church and of the Post-Apostolic Age. The name of Jesus was still included in the earliest threefold formula, which was introduced in the Age of the Greek Apologists and used in the early Old Catholic Age. Early trinitarians in the Old Catholic Age such as Tertullian and Origen omitted the name of Jesus altogether, using the titles of Father, Son, and Holy Spirit.

The common pastors and laity were not as quick to

change the baptismal formula. Various popular writings and the *Treatise on Rebaptism* indicate that in the first part of the Old Catholic Age the Jesus Name formula was still dominant and that in the latter part of the age it was still widespread. The *Treatise on Rebaptism* and the controversy between Cyprian and Stephen reveal that both splinter groups and groups within the institutional church still practiced baptism in the name of Jesus throughout the age.

Clearly, the Jesus Name formula was not replaced overnight. Even when theologians began to advocate the trinitarian formula, they were careful to affirm respect for the original and still popular formula. Gradually, during a time of coexistence and compromise, the trinitarian formula gained ascendancy and eventually replaced the Jesus Name formula in the institutional church.

Evidently, the primary impetus for the newer formula was controversy over the Godhead. Trinitarian theologians began to emphasize the trinitarian formula as a means of combatting first modalism and then Arianism. By the end of the age the trinitarian formula had become dominant.

9

Oneness Concepts in Popular Belief

As we have seen, the theologians of the Old Catholic Age whose writings remain were predominantly trinitarian of one sort or another. As chapter 1 discussed, however, it is difficult to know just how representative these existing writings are and how many works that taught other views have been lost to us. We may never be able to reconstruct an accurate picture of the age as a whole.

Nevertheless, it is evident that Oneness views were prevalent in the Old Catholic Age, particularly among the common believers. Oneness concepts appeared in the popular writings of the age, among the Montanists, and in the teachings of a prominent group that historians call the modalistic monarchians, or modalists.

Chapter 10 will analyze the doctrine of the modalistic teachers in detail, but for the purposes of this chapter we will use the term *modalism* in a generic sense to refer to a system of belief that simultaneously affirms the numerical oneness of God (to the exclusion of trinitarianism) and the absolute deity of Jesus Christ.

Oneness Views in Popular Literature

Although theologians during the Old Catholic Age began to speak in trinitarian terms, it appears that for many decades most believers continued to think and speak in terms of a basic, original Oneness belief.

To obtain a glimpse of prevalent views among the common people as distinguished from theologians and philosophers, of necessity we must quote primarily from apocryphal, anonymous, or pseudonymous books. We do not endorse these writings or all their contents, but in an incidental way the quotations show popular modes of thought.

The following quotations from popular Christian literature of the time indicate that many people thought of Jesus as the incarnation of the fullness of the one God. By "popular" we mean primarily "of the common people" and in a secondary sense "accepted among people in general; common; prevalent; liked by very many or most people."

The Testaments of the Twelve Patriarchs (second century): "The Lord God, the Mighty One of Israel, . . . appear[ed] upon earth as a man. . . . God hath taken a body and eaten with men and saved men" (2:6).

Acts of Peter and Paul: Paul "gave thanks to the Lord and Master Jesus Christ," and Christian Gentiles told their Jewish counterparts, "We . . . believe to be a Saviour the God whom you have forsaken in unbelief."

Acts of Peter and Andrew: "Truly great is the God of Peter and Andrew, and I from this time forth believe in the name of our Lord Jesus Christ."

Acts of John: "He . . . is higher and more exalted than every name that we speak of—our God, Jesus Christ."

This work includes a prayer to "God Lord Jesus Christ" and other prayers "in the name of Jesus Christ" but no trinitarian prayers. It also contains a Eucharistic prayer, which does not address Father, Son, and Holy Spirit as trinitarian Eucharistic prayers do, but instead addresses the Lord and describes Him as the one God revealed through His Son. "We glorify the name by which Thou has been called by the Father; we glorify the name by which thou hast been called through the Son; we glorify the resurrection which has been manifested to us through Thee; of Thee we glorify . . . Him called Son of man for our sakes, the truth, the rest, the knowledge, the freedom, the place of refuge in Thee. For Thou alone art Lord, the root of immortality, and the fountain of incorruption, and the seat of the ages; Thou who hast been called all these for our sakes, that now we, calling upon Thee through these, may recognize Thine illimitable presence, that can be seen only by the pure, seen in Thine only Son."

The way in which these statements are woven into the text without explanation indicates that the authors simply assumed their view of God and Christ to be the accepted one. They did not see these Oneness statements as innovative, controversial, questionable, or confusing. They took for granted that their readers would understand and agree, and they probably did not even consciously think about the matter.

Historians today generally conclude that the common people of the Old Catholic Age thought in modalistic rather than consciously trinitarian terms.[1] The following quotation describes the most common way in which modern trinitarian historians try to explain the prevalence of modalism or monarchianism in the Roman Empire.

Perhaps the most popular contemporary explanation for this phenomena is that which sees the popular monarchian movement as being an initial reaction of the common Christians against the philosophical articulation of the common trinitarian creed and liturgy of the Church. On this view, the Church had always confessed a faith in the Father, Son and Holy Spirit, but had, with the exception of a few theologians (e.g. the Apologists), never explained, or even attempted to explain, this faith. . . . It had never occurred to most Christians, including most of the Church's leaders, that there was anything to be explained in the Church's triadic confession and liturgy prior to this late second-century controversy. It was only when the more educated among them began to attempt to think through this confession, largely in philosophical categories which were not familiar to the common Christians, that the problem of how God could be one and yet, in some sense, three first arose. It was in reaction to the initial solutions proposed by such educated leaders as Tertullian and Hippolytus that the modalistic monarchian interpretation of the faith was born. The church leaders' interpretation emphasized the plurality of the Church's confession, and tended towards subordinationism and/or tritheism. The common Christians of Rome, in contrast, opted for a theory which emphasized the unity and singularity of God in the Church's creed and liturgy as well as the centrality of Christ in their worship.[2]

When we examine the New Testament and the Post-Apostolic Age it does not appear that the earliest creed, confession, liturgy, or faith of the church was primarily triadic or threefold with respect to God's being. Nevertheless, this explanation offers insight into the predominance of modalism and the conflict between modalism and trinitarianism.

Oneness Views among the Montanists

At the beginning of the Old Catholic Age, around 177, a group called the Montanists were expelled from the institutional church. The Montanists emphasized the work and gifts of the Spirit, including speaking in tongues; the priesthood of all believers; the imminent return of Jesus Christ; and a life of strict morality, which later tended to legalism and asceticism. They were accused of teaching that their founder, Montanus, was the incarnation of the Holy Spirit, but apparently this charge arose because he gave divine prophecies in the first person.

The doctrine of the trinity was in its formative stages when the Montanists split away, so it is unlikely that the early Montanists were trinitarian. Later, some of them apparently embraced trinitarianism, and indeed a noted convert to Montanism, Tertullian, was later instrumental in developing the doctrine. It is not clear whether his trinitarian ideas were shaped in part by Montanism or whether he was largely responsible for injecting trinitarian ideas into Montanism.

The historical evidence indicates that many of the Montanists—perhaps all of them originally—did not adhere to a concept of plural persons in the Godhead but affirmed the absolute deity of Jesus. Didymus stated that the church did not recognize the baptism of the Montanists because they held to modalism and did not baptize in the three persons of the trinity (*On the Trinity*, 2:15).[3] Apparently, they used the Jesus Name formula. The Council of Constantinople identified the Montanists as modalists (canon 7).[4] Hippolytus twice identified some of the Montanists as modalists (*Refutation of All Heresies* 8:12; 10:22). And according to Pseudo-Tertullian in *Against All Heresies*, one group of Montanists were modalists (7:2).[5]

Jaroslav Pekilan concluded that some Montanists as well as many other Christians embraced a form of modalism.

> One party among the Montanists . . . [seems] to have embraced the doctrine that Father, Son, and Holy Spirit were only successive modes of manifestation of the one God. . . . Such language about the Trinity was in itself quite acceptable in the second century, and even later. . . . [Thus] some Montanists held to a naive formula for the Trinity that was shared by other Christians.[6]

Modalistic Monarchianism

The most significant movement for our discussion is what historians call modalistic monarchianism, or modalism. The label means that Father, Son, and Holy Spirit are modes (manifestations, not persons) of the Monarchy (the one sovereign God). "Modalistic monarchianism, conceiving that the whole fulness of the Godhead dwelt in Christ, took exception to the 'subordination' of some church writers and maintained that the names Father and Son were only different designations of the same subject, the one God, who 'with reference to the relations in which He had previously stood to the world is called the Father, but in reference to His appearance in humanity is called the Son.'"[7]

The practical effect of this doctrine was to emphasize both the absolute oneness of God and the absolute deity of Jesus Christ. The modalists viewed "Jesus as the incarnation of the Godhead" and "the Father incarnate."[8] According to Heick, they rejected the Logos-Christology of trinitarianism as Gnostic, and "the chief interest of Modalism was to maintain Christian monotheism without sacrificing the divinity of Christ."[9]

Pelikan views modalism as the logical expression of the existing faith of the average Christian. "Modalistic Monarchianism . . . may be defined as an effort to provide a theology for the language of devotion. . . . Both monotheism and the deity of Christ were safeguarded. . . . This doctrine of the relation between Christ and God turns out to have been a systematization of popular Christian belief."[10]

The most prominent exponents of modalism known to us were Praxeas of Asia Minor, Noetus of Smyrna, and Sabellius of Libya. They taught in Rome in the late second and early third century. Other modalists were Epigonus, a disciple of Noetus; Cleomenes, a disciple of Epigonus; and probably Commodian, a North African bishop. In addition, it appears that at least three Roman bishops— Victor, Zephyrinus, and Callistus—embraced this view.

According to the renowned historian Adolph Harnack, modalism was the official theory in Rome for almost a generation, was at one time "embraced by the great majority of all Christians," and was the most dangerous rival to trinitarianism from 180 to 300.[11] Heick concurred: "Modalism became very widespread and influential in the

West . . . . The doctrine that God *in toto* was incarnate in Jesus . . . was the dangerous opponent of the Logos-Christology between A.D. 180 and A.D. 300."[12]

Why was modalism not mentioned or not "dangerous" earlier? As this chapter and chapter 10 document, basic Oneness belief was predominant everywhere in earlier times; and as chapters 4, 5, 6, 7, and 11 document, trinitarianism was just developing around 180. Therefore, before 180 there was no significant controversy over the trinity, and no modalistic teachers were singled out for attack.

Dynamic Monarchianism

Historians distinguish the modalistic monarchian teachers from other teachers they call the dynamic monarchians although, as the labels indicate, both sets of teachers defended God's oneness against trinitarianism. Of the two, the modalists were far more numerous and influential. Philip Schaff explained the difference:

> The rationalistic or dynamic Monarchians . . . denied the divinity of Christ, or explained it as a mere 'power' (*dunamis*). . . . Modalistic Monarchians . . . identified the Son with the Father, and admitted at most only a modal trinity, that is a threefold mode of revelation, but not a tripersonality. . . . The latter was by far the more profound and Christian, and accordingly met with the greater acceptance.[13]

The following teachers are usually identified as dynamic monarchians: Theodotus of Byzantium; Artemon of Syria; Paul of Samosata, bishop of Antioch, its most noted exponent; and perhaps an early group known as the Alogi. Louis Berkhof described Paul's views as follows:

> The Logos was indeed *homoouios* or consubstantial with the Father, but was not a distinct Person in the Godhead. He could be identified with God, because He existed in Him just as human reason exists in man. He was merely an impersonal power, present in all men, but particularly operative in the *man* Jesus. By penetrating the humanity of Jesus progressively, as it did that of no other man, this divine power gradually deified it. And because the man Jesus was thus deified, He is worthy of divine honour, though He cannot be regarded as God in the strict sense of the word.[14]

Paul's opponent Malchion charged in his *Epistle against Paul of Samosata* (270): "He put a stop to psalms sung in honour of Jesus" (2).

William Chalfant suggested that the dynamic monarchians may have held a form of Oneness belief but their trinitarian opponents misunderstood their emphasis on the true humanity of Jesus, which is essential to a consistent Oneness theology.[15] While this suggestion is intriguing, it seems doubtful, at least based on existing evidence (which is admittedly indirect and fragmentary). The sources for information about these people are even more meager that the sources for the modalists, but it seems that dynamic monarchianism was similar to Unitarianism. As it has been described to us by ancient writers, it is incompatible with modern Oneness, so we will not investigate it further.

Evidence from Origen

Origen (died 254) of Alexandria was well acquainted with modalistic belief and opposed it vehemently. He taught that the Word in John 1:1 was a distinct person from the Father, but in his *Commentary on John* he admitted that most Christians did not agree. Like Tertullian, he attributed their belief to stupidity, although he also spoke of scholars who opposed his view.

"I am often led to wonder when I consider the things that are said about Christ, even by those who are in earnest in their belief in Him. . . . But when they come to the title Logos (Word), and repeat that Christ alone is the Word of God, they are not consistent, and do not, as in the case of the other titles, search out what is behind the meaning of the term 'Word.' I wonder at the stupidity of the general run of Christian in this matter. I do not mince matters; it is nothing but stupidity. . . . One of the names applied to the Saviour is that which He Himself does not utter, but which John records;—the Word who was in the beginning with God, God the Word. And it is worth our while to fix our attention for a moment on those scholars who omit consideration of most of the great names we have mentioned and regard this as the most important one. . . . They imagine the Son of God to be the utterance of the Father deposited, as it were, in syllables, and accordingly they do not allow Him, if we examine them farther, any independent hypostasis [personhood], nor are they clear about His essence. I do not mean that they confuse its qualities, but the fact of His having an essence of His own. For no one can understand how that which is said to be 'Word' can be a Son. And such an animated Word, not being a separate entity from the Father, accordingly as it, having no subsistence, is not a Son" (1:23).

Commenting on the last portion of John 1:1, Origen wrote, "Now there are many who are sincerely concerned about religion, and who fall here into great perplexity. They are afraid that they may be proclaiming two Gods, and their fear drives them into doctrines which are false and wicked. Either they deny that the Son has a distinct nature of His own besides that of the Father, and make Him whom they call the Son to be God all but the name, or they deny the divinity of the Son" (2:2).

Origen identified four classes of people who believe in God, two of which are significant to our discussion. The first class is those who have faith in both God and the Word; the second is those "who know nothing but Jesus Christ and Him crucified, considering that the Word made flesh is the whole Word, and knowing only Christ after the flesh. Such is the great multitude of those who are counted believers" (2:3). "God the Logos is God, perhaps of those who attribute everything to Him and who consider Him to be their Father" (2:3).

Origen acknowledged that some people used John 2:19 to show "that the Son did not differ in number from the Father, but that both were one, not only in point of substance but in point of subject, and that the Father and the Son were said to be different in some of their aspects but not in their hypostases [persons]" (10:21).

Origen responded to the anti-Christian work of a pagan named Celsus, and in his tract *Against Celsus* he recorded much of Celsus's comments about Christianity. In arguing against Christianity Celsus described its doctrine of God in modalistic terms, obviously thinking he was accurately characterizing its belief. "He describes our answer in the following terms: 'Since God is great and difficult to see, He put His own Spirit into a body that resembled ours, and sent it down to us, that we might be enabled to hear Him and become acquainted with Him'" (6:69).

Origen acknowledged to Celsus that modalistic beliefs were common in Christendom. "[Some] deny that the Father and the Son are two persons" (8:12). "There may be some individuals among the multitudes of believers who are not in entire agreement with us, and who incautiously assert that the Saviour is the Most High God; however, we do not hold with them" (8:14). Origen made this admission to pagans he was trying to convert, although a proselyter usually does not disclose what he considers to be aberrant views within his own ranks. Evidently, modalism was so widespread that even its strongest opponents could not successfully push it into obscurity.

His *Commentary on Titus* also describes the belief: "They do not wish to seem to affirm two gods; they do not wish to deny the divinity of the Saviour; then they end by admitting merely two names, and one single person."[16]

In *On Prayer* Origen objected to the prevalent practice of praying directly to Jesus Christ instead of to the Father through the Son.

Commodian

Commodian was apparently a North African bishop who wrote around 240, and it seems that he had a modalistic concept of God. If so, he was the only modalist from this age to have some of his writings preserved.

Instructions for the Christian Life speaks of "the almighty God, the living Christ" (42) and "God-Christ" (80). *Apologetic Poem Against Jews and Gentiles* calls Christ "God Himself."[17] Commodian also wrote, "The Father went into the Son, one God everywhere."[18]

Conclusions

Despite the limitations and uncertainties associated with our study, a careful analysis of the existing writings reveals that the majority of believers during much of the Old Catholic Age did not think in trinitarian terms but affirmed the numerical oneness of God and the absolute deity of Jesus Christ.

It is difficult to be more precise in describing these beliefs. In the case of the popular literature, we have only brief statements in passing, not a systematic theology. In the case of the Montanists, we have only secondary sources. Origen's writings show us that many people rejected his teaching in favor of Oneness concepts, but again, evidence from him is secondary. Commodian is a primary source, but his existing works only touch briefly upon the doctrine of God.

This is not to say that nothing of substance was written to teach Oneness concepts. To the contrary, Origen mentioned "scholars" who advanced a Oneness concept of the Word. He would hardly have called them scholars, especially when he was trying to disparage their views, unless the fact of their scholarship was undisputed and well known. It is safe to assume, then, that in this age Oneness views were expressed in scholarly study and exposition, both oral and written. But given the eventual triumph of trinitarianism, it is understandable that little primary evidence remains of Oneness concepts even though they were first dominant and later still prevalent in the Old Catholic Age.

The most fruitful area available to us for the investigation of Oneness concepts during this time is the teaching of the modalists. Although no writings of the leading modalists have survived, Tertullian, Hippolytus, and to a lesser extent, Novatian have given us descriptions of their doctrine. Chapter 10 analyzes the major modalistic teachers to ascertain what they believed and to compare their doctrine to modern Oneness.

10

Teachers of Modalism:
Praxeas, Noetus, and Sabellius

From our discussion to this point, it appears that in the Old Catholic Age the strongest and clearest Oneness concepts were expressed by teachers whom historians call the modalistic monarchians or modalists. Chapter 9 has briefly defined their basic position. We now turn to an examination of the specific beliefs of the leading modalistic teachers in an attempt to determine how their doctrine compares to modern Oneness.

Since none of the writings of the major teachers of modalism have survived, we must attempt to determine their views by reading the works of their opponents, a method that presents several difficulties. First, the record is scanty, and it is not sufficient to give us definitive information on many points. Second, we must take the doctrinal biases of the opponents into consideration. Deliberately or through lack of understanding, they may have distorted or misrepresented the views of the modalists. Third, in some cases we must rely heavily on descriptions written in the fourth century, a century or more after the major modalistic teachers lived. In the intervening time, much information was probably lost or garbled in transmission, and on many points the descriptions probably reflect the views of fourth-century people who opposed trinitarianism in one way or another and were accused of modalism.

We should also keep in mind the following caveat relative to our two primary sources:

> We know of this conflict only through Hippolytus and Tertullian, two impassioned controversialists: when they wrote the books upon which we have to rely, Hippolytus was a schismatic and head of a little church in Rome, and Tertullian was a Montanist, a violent opponent of the church of the "psychics" and of the bishop of Rome.[1]

Praxeas

Our information about Praxeas comes from *Against Praxeas* by Tertullian. Since the name Praxeas can mean "busybody," it is possible that Tertullian used a fictitious name for his opponent. Perhaps he was a prominent or popular leader whom Tertullian could not successfully attack openly, possibly the bishop of Rome, Zephyrinus. Although Roman residents familiar with the controversy surely knew whom Tertullian meant, perhaps believers in other areas did not. If Praxeas was highly regarded in various areas of the empire, perhaps Tertullian did not have much hope of success in opposing him directly but felt that he could achieve more by denouncing Praxeas's doctrine without mentioning the man's real name.

According to Tertullian's report, Praxeas came from Asia Minor to Rome about 190 and taught his doctrine there. The doctrine spread everywhere, including Carthage, and stirred up a great controversy. Under pressure,

Praxeas supposedly signed a retraction, but the doctrine sprang up again about twenty years later, which caused Tertullian to write his tract. References in *Against Praxeas* 1 and *Against All Heresies* 8 by Pseudo-Tertullian indicate that Victor, bishop of Rome (189-99), supported the teaching of Praxeas. Evidently, the Roman church already had the basic concept before the time of Praxeas, so that he was readily received when he arrived there.

Against Praxeas reveals that the doctrine existed everywhere: "The tares of Praxeas had then everywhere shaken out their seed" (1). In a sarcastic and condescending passage, Tertullian admitted that most Christians embraced this doctrine and opposed trinitarianism on the ground that it destroyed monotheism. "The simple, indeed, I will not call them unwise and unlearned, who always constitute the majority of believers, are startled at the dispensation (of the Three in One), on the ground that their very rule of faith withdraws them from the world's plurality of gods to the one only true God; not understanding that, although He is the one only God, He must yet be believed in with His own oikonomia [economy, dispensation]. The numerical order and distribution of the Trinity they assume to be a division of the Unity" (3).

Significantly, the "majority of believers" opposed trinitarianism. Tertullian tried to explain away this uncomfortable fact by arguing that, after all, the majority of believers are always simple and, if the truth were known, ignorant.

In rejecting trinitarianism, they appealed to the "rule of faith"—a confession of basic doctrine, probably a confession made at baptism. In *Against Heresies* Irenaeus quoted the rule of faith as teaching one God the Father, the incarnation of Christ Jesus the Son of God, and the gift of the Holy Spirit (1:10:1; 3:6:4). Either the church did not regard this statement as trinitarian at all, or else Irenaeus did not truly record the earliest rule of faith. The central tenet of the earliest Christian confession was evidently God's oneness, not a statement of threeness.

Praxeas and his followers emphasized God's oneness and complained that Tertullian and his followers taught two or three gods. "They are constantly throwing out against us that we are preachers of two gods and three gods, while they take to themselves pre-eminently the credit of being worshippers of the One God; just as if the Unity itself with irrational deductions did not produce heresy, and the Trinity rationally considered [did not] constitute the truth. We, say they, maintain the Monarchy (or, sole government of God)" (3). In support of this teaching, the modalists cited passages such as Isaiah 44:6 and 45:5, 18.

In particular, the modalists objected to the concept of a plurality of persons and maintained that Father, Son, and Spirit were three titles of one God. "[They think] that one cannot believe in One Only God in any other way than by saying that the Father, the Son, and the Holy Ghost are the very selfsame Person" (2). "They contend for the identity of the Father and Son and Spirit" (9).

Praxeas emphasized the full deity of Jesus Christ and used passages such as John 10:30 and John 14:9-10 to identify Him as the Father incarnate. "He maintains that there is one only Lord, the Almighty Creator of the world, in order that out of this doctrine of the unity he may fabricate a heresy. He says that the Father Himself came down into the Virgin, was Himself born of her, Himself suffered, indeed was Himself Jesus Christ" (1). "God Himself, the Lord Almighty, . . . in their preaching they declare to be Jesus Christ" (2). "You make Christ to be the Father" (28).

He denied that the Word was a second person. "You will not allow [the Word] to be really a substantive being, by having a substance of His own; in such a way that He may be regarded as an objective thing and a person, and so be able (as being constituted second to God the Father,) to make two, the Father and the Son, God and the Word. For you will say, what is a word, but a voice and sound of the mouth" (7).

Likewise, he denied that the Father and the Son were two persons. Instead, "Father" refers to the one God in His invisible divine nature, but according to Luke 1:35, "Son" refers to His manifestation in flesh. "[Praxeas maintains] that He is invisible as the Father, and visible as the Son" (14). "He was visible indeed in the flesh, but was invisible before His appearance in the flesh; so that He who as the Father was invisible before the flesh, is the same as the Son who was visible in the flesh" (15). "All in one Person, they distinguish two, Father and Son, understanding the Son to be flesh, that is man, that is Jesus; and the Father to be spirit, that is God, that is Christ. . . . See, say they, it was announced by the angel: 'Therefore that Holy Thing which shall be born of thee shall be called the Son of God.' Therefore, (they argue,) as it was the flesh that was born, it must be the flesh that is the Son of God" (27).

Praxeas said the Holy Spirit is not a third person; rather, the title refers to the one God's nature as Spirit. According to John 4:24, the Father is the Spirit. "You insist upon it that the Father Himself is the Spirit, on the ground that 'God is a Spirit'" (27).

Praxeas apparently taught that the name of Jesus fully reveals God, which would indicate that he baptized in the name of Jesus. Tertullian wrote, "They more readily supposed that the Father acted in the Son's name. . . . The point maintained by them [is] that the name of Christ belongs also to the Father" (17).

In response to the modalists, Tertullian quoted many passages of Scripture to show a distinction between the Father and the Son. He stated that he would prefer to believe in two gods than in their kind of God. "Were we even to maintain that they are two separate gods, as you are so fond of throwing out against us, it would be a more tolerable assertion than the maintenance of so versatile and changeful a God as yours!" (23).

Tertullian's most famous charge against Praxeas was that his doctrine made the Father suffer and die. Since Greek philosophy taught that God was impassible (incapable of suffering), to many people this charge sounded quite damaging. It shows, however, that the early trinitarians did not believe in the full deity of Jesus Christ, for if it was abhorrent to think of God the Father suffering, why was it not equally abhorrent to think of "God the Son" suffering? In contrast to these trinitarians, in the Post-Apostolic Age Clement of Rome and Ignatius wrote about God's sufferings in Christ.

Tertullian's accusation caused the Praxeans to be labeled Patripassians, which comes from Latin words meaning "the Father suffered." Some historians still use this label for modalism, but Praxeas denied that the Father died as to His deity. He explained that Christ died as to His humanity only—as the Son—but Tertullian refused to listen. "Very well, say you; since we on our side affirm our doctrine in precisely the same terms which you use on your side respecting the Son, we are not guilty of blasphemy against the Lord God, for we do not maintain that He died after the divine nature, but only after the human. Nay, but you do blaspheme; because you allege not only that the Father died, but that He died the death of the cross. . . . They grant us so far that the Father and the Son are Two; adding that, since it is the Son indeed who suffers, the Father is only His fellow-sufferer" (29).

In concluding his polemic, Tertullian accused Praxeas of a Jewish concept of God, asserting that the doctrine of the trinity was necessary to separate Judaism from Christianity. "But, (this doctrine of yours bears a likeness) to the Jewish faith. . . . Now, what difference would there be between us and them, if there were not this distinction, which you are for breaking down?" (31).

Noetus, Zephyrinus, and Callistus

Our information about Noetus comes from Hippolytus. Noetus was from Smyrna in Asia Minor, and he founded a theological school in Rome. His followers included Epigonus, Cleomenes, and Sabellius. Hippolytus bitterly charged the two Roman bishops after Victor Zephyrinus (199-217) and Callistus (217-23)—with promoting the views of Noetus. Callistus excommunicated both Hippolytus and Sabellius.

In *The Refutation of All Heresies* Hippolytus acknowledged how widespread the doctrine of Noetus was, saying, "no one is ignorant" of it (9:5). Moreover, he stated that because of the two Roman bishops' help, this doctrine was able to "prevail" (9:2).

Like Praxeas, Noetus emphasized the absolute oneness of God and denied that the Father and the Son were two persons. Instead, "Father" and "Son" refer to the same being but in different manifestations. "Noetus affirms that the Son and the Father are the same" (9:5). "For in this manner he thinks to establish the sovereignty of God, alleging that Father and Son, so called, are one and the same (substance), not one individual produced from a different one, but Himself from Himself; and that He is styled by name Father and Son, according to the vicissitude of times" (9:5). "Noetus asserts that there is one Father and God of the universe, and that He made all things. . . . And the Noetians suppose that this Father Himself is called Son, (and vice versa,) in reference to the events which at their own proper periods happen to them severally" (10:23).

Specifically, the title "Son" relates to the Incarnation. Hippolytus reported the position of Noetus on this point while distorting it to make it sound absurd. "When indeed, then, the Father had not been born, He yet was justly styled Father; and when it pleased Him to undergo generation, having been begotten, He Himself became His own Son, not another's" (9:5).

Similarly, Callistus explained that "Father, Son, and Spirit" are three titles of one being. "Son" refers to the humanity of Christ, and the divine Spirit in Christ is actually the Father, the Word, the Holy Spirit.

"Callistus alleges that the Logos Himself is Son, and that Himself is Father; and that though denominated by a different title, yet that in reality He is one indivisible spirit. And he maintains that the Father is not one person and the Son another, but that they are one and the same. . . . And he affirms that the Spirit, which became incarnate in the virgin, is not different from the Father, but one and the same. . . . For that which is seen, which is man, he considers to be the Son; whereas the Spirit, which was contained in the Son, to be the Father. 'For,' says (Callistus), 'I will not profess belief in two Gods, Father and Son, but in one. For the Father, who subsisted in the Son Himself, after He had taken unto Himself our flesh, raised it to the nature of Deity, by bringing it into union with Himself, and made it one; so that Father and Son must be styled one God, and that this Person being one, cannot be two.'" (9:8). "For Spirit, as the Deity, is, he says, not any being different from the Logos, or the Logos from the Deity; therefore this one person, (according to Callistus,) is divided nominally, but substantially not so. He supposes this one Logos to be God, and affirms that there was in the case of the Word an incarnation" (9:23).

In *Against the Heresy of One Noetus* Hippolytus repeated Tertullian's accusation of Patripassianism. "[Noetus] alleged that Christ was the Father Himself, and that the Father Himself was born, and suffered, and died" (1). Noetus explained, "Christ suffered, being Himself God; and consequently the Father suffered, for He was the Father Himself" (2).

According to Hippolytus's *Refutation*, Zephyrinus and Callistus responded much as Praxeas had, explaining that Christ suffered as to His humanity—as the Son. Since the deity (Father) dwelt in the Son, the most that could be said was that the Father suffered with the Son. "[Zephyrinus said,] 'I know that there is one God, Jesus Christ; nor except Him do I know any other that is begotten and amenable to suffering. . . . The Father did not die, but the Son'" (9:6). "Callistus contends that the Father suffered along with the Son; for he does not wish to assert that the Father suffered" (9:8). "He is disposed (to maintain), that He who was seen in the flesh and was crucified is Son, but that the Father it is who dwells in Him" (9:23).

Because of this explanation, Hippolytus accused Callistus of compromising modalism and combining it with the doctrine of Theodotus, a dynamic monarchian. Consequently, some historians divide the modalists into two different categories: those who said the Father suffered (Patripassians) and those who said the Father only suffered with the Son. It is possible that Noetus held to an unsophisticated form of modalism, but it seems more likely that the views of Callistus and Noetus were compatible, for Praxeas had earlier given much the same explanation, and the identification of the Son with the humanity of Christ is essential to any consistent form of Oneness. Moreover, Hippolytus definitely wished to paint the worst possible picture of Callistus, and one way he did so was to accuse him of dishonesty and compromise.

At the same time, it is possible that Callistus was guilty of compromise in some way, for according to Hippolytus, he excommunicated Sabellius and was accused by him of having "transgressed his first faith" (9:7).

Hippolytus's linking of Callistus with Theodotus is a point in favor of Chalfant's speculation that Theodotus and the dynamic monarchians were closer to Oneness than history has portrayed them. If Hippolytus misunderstood Callistus's doctrine of the Son, perhaps he and other trinitarians misunderstood Theodotus as well.

The allies of Noetus accused Hippolytus of polytheism.

"[Zephyrinus] called us worshippers of two gods" (9:6). "[Callistus] reproach[ed] to us, 'Ye are Ditheists'" (9:8).

In *Against Noetus*, Hippolytus reported that Noetus used the following passages of Scripture to support his doctrine: Exodus 3:6; 20:3; Isaiah 44:6; 45:14; John 10:30; 14:9; Romans 9:5.

Noetus protested against the trinitarian use of "Son" and "Word" as equivalent in terminology and denied that the Word was a second person. "But some one will say to me, You adduce a thing strange to me, when you call the Son the Word. For John indeed speaks of the Word, but it is by a figure of speech" (15).

Noetus affirmed the full deity of Jesus Christ and his identity as the Father incarnate. "He alleged that Christ was the Father Himself' (1). "[They say,] If therefore I acknowledge Christ to be God, He is the Father Himself, if He is indeed God" (2). "You see, then, he says, that this is God, who is the only One, and who afterward did show Himself, and conversed with men." (2). When Noetus met with his opponents, he asked, "What evil, then, am I doing in glorifying Christ?" (1).

In recording the statements of Zephyrinus on this subject, Hippolytus has given us the oldest known doctrinal pronouncement of a Roman bishop. Ironically, the Roman Catholic Church, which is trinitarian, considers Zephyrinus to be a pope, and it holds that an official doctrinal pronouncement by a pope is infallible. At least two Roman bishops endorsed modalism—Zephyrinus and Callistus and no doubt they considered their position to be consistent with all the bishops before their time. Sometime later, another Roman bishop, Stephen, still endorsed baptism in the name of Jesus. (See chapter 8.)

Sabellius

Sabellius was apparently the most prominent modalist teacher, for in later times the modalists became known as Sabellians and the Nicene and post-Nicene writers referred primarily to him. Yet we know less about him than we do about Praxeas and Noetus, and what we know of him is primarily from fourth-century writers such as Athanasius and the Cappadocians, who wrote well over one hundred years after his ministry. In many cases it seems that these writers described people in their own time who either called themselves Sabellians or were accused of Sabellianism, instead of the views of Sabellius himself.

Sabellius probably came from Libya. He apparently preached in Rome about 215, during the time of Zephyrinus and Callistus. According to Hippolytus, he was excommunicated by Callistus, who nevertheless adhered to a form of modalism also and who excommunicated Hippolytus as well. If this report is true, perhaps Callistus expelled both men as a compromise to bring harmony, or perhaps he objected to some points in the theology of Sabellius. Later, "Sabellius was condemned by a Council held at Rome, probably in 258; again at Nicea [325], and again at Constantinople [381], where Sabellian baptism was pronounced invalid."[2]

From the descriptions of later writers, it seems that Sabellius affirmed the same points as the earlier modalists with a possible addition: he may have taught that the manifestations of Father, Son, and Spirit were strictly successive and did not occur simultaneously. If so, in this respect he does not represent the views of the older modalists or of modern Oneness. Pelikan said it is "somewhat dubious" as to whether Sabellius actually taught this point.[3] It is easy to see how trinitarians could have misunderstand his explanation of the progressive revelation of Father, Son, and Spirit in redemptive history (Father in creation, Son in redemption, Holy Spirit in regeneration) and not realize that these roles could be simultaneous as well. On the other hand, it is difficult to see how anyone could argue that these roles are strictly successive in light of scriptural passages that mention two or more simultaneously.

The following descriptions summarize what is typically said of Sabellius.

> God is a Unity (*Monas*). There are no distinctions in the divine Being, but God the divine Unity reveals himself successively in three different modes or forms (*onomata, prosopa*) [names, faces]. In the Father, God reveals himself as creator; in the Son, as redeemer; and in the Spirit, as sanctifier. These are not three hypostases [persons]; they are rather three roles or parts played by the one person. In other words, all three are one and the same person. . . . After the *prosopon* of the Father accomplished its work in the giving of the law, it fell back into its original condition. Advancing again through the incarnation as Son, it returned by the ascension into the absolute being of the Monad. It revealed itself finally as the Holy Spirit, to return again, after securing the perfect sanctification of the Church, into the Monad that knows no distinctions, there to abide through all eternity. Sabellius characterized this process as an expansion and contraction.[4]

It is hard to determine in detail just what he taught. It is perfectly clear, however, that he distinguished between the unity of the divine essence and the plurality of its manifestation, which are represented as following one another like the parts of a drama. Sabellius indeed sometimes spoke of three divine persons, but then used the word "person" in the original sense of the word, in which it signifies a role of acting or a mode of manifestation. According to him the names Father, Son and Holy Spirit are simply designations of three different phases under which the one divine essence manifests itself. God reveals Himself as the Father in creation and in the giving of the law, as Son in the incarnation, and as Holy Spirit in regeneration and sanctification.[5]

Athanasius recorded that when Bishop Dionysius of Alexandria wrote against the Sabellians the doctrine was widespread: "At that date certain of the Bishops in Pentapolis, Upper Libya, held with Sabellius. And they were so successful with their opinions that the Son of God was scarcely any longer preached in the churches" (*On the Opinion of Dionysius* 5).

Like the earlier modalists, Sabellius insisted upon the absolute oneness of God and taught that the Father and Son were not two persons. Athanasius said the Sabellians spoke of "a Son-Father" (*huiopater*), describing him as "one essence" (*monoousion*) instead of two persons of "same essence" (*homoousion*) (*Statement of Faith* 2). He described the Sabellians of his day as follows: "Those who say that the Father and Son and Holy Ghost are the same, and irreligiously take the Three Names of one and the same Reality and Person, we justly proscribe from the Church, because they suppose the illimitable and impassible Father to be limitable withal and passible through His becoming man: for such are they whom Romans call Patripassians, and we Sabellians" (*On Synods* 2:6). According to *Discourse against the Arians* 3:4, Sabellius was judged a heretic for saying "that the Same becomes at one time Father, at another His own Son" (3:4), and Sabellius said the "Father and Son are the same" (4:2:2).

Pseudo-Athanasius recorded the doctrine of expansion and contraction in *Orations against the Arians*. "Sabellius also raves in saying . . . 'the Father is the same, but is dilated into Son and Spirit'" (4:25). *A Sectional Confession of Faith* wrongly attributed to Gregory Thaumaturgus likewise explains: "Sabellius . . . says that the Father and the Son are the same. For he holds that the Father is he who speaks, and that the Son is the Word that abides in the Father, and becomes manifest at the time of the creation, and thereafter reverts to God on the fulfilling of all things. The same affirmation he makes also of the Spirit" (7).

Basil gave a similar description of Sabellius's view. "The same God, being one in matter, was metamorphosed as the need of the moment required, and spoken of now as Father, now as Son, and now as Holy Ghost" (*Letters* 210). In the same letter Basil argued against the Sabellians that Matthew 28:19 records three names, not one. "It is obvious, they urge, that the name is one, for it is not 'in the names,' but 'in the name.' . . . We must not suppose that here one name is delivered to us. . . . These are different names." Moreover, he argued that the name described by Acts 4:12 is "Son of God." This discussion indicates that the Sabellians probably baptized in the name of Jesus, linking the one name of Matthew 28:19 with the name of Jesus in Acts 4:12.

Basil further explained that according to Sabellius "the name of Son" represents God in "a descent to human interests" (214).

Like the earlier modalists, Sabellius did not equate Logos with Son in terminology but said the Logos was clothed with the Son.[6] And like them he denied that the Father died as to His deity.[7] This position indicates that he did not regard Father and Son as strictly successive but as simultaneous after the Incarnation, for He apparently held that Jesus died as the Son but the divine nature incarnate in Jesus—the Father—did not die.

The contemporary sources that we have for Sabellius are Hippolytus, who referred to him briefly, and possibly Novatian. Novatian described later modalists, who were evidently Sabellians. Significantly, Novatian's description sounds much like the earlier accounts of Tertullian and Hippolytus. Neither he nor Hippolytus mentioned the questionable doctrine later attributed to Sabellius of successive manifestations by expansion and contraction.

In his *Treatise concerning the Trinity* Novatian acknowledged that the modalists were very numerous and used this fact to argue in favor of the deity of Christ. "Many heretics, moved by the magnitude and truth of this divinity, exaggerating His honours above measure, have dared to announce or to think Him not the Son, but God the Father Himself. And this, although it is contrary to the truth of the Scriptures, is still a great and excellent argument for the divinity of Christ, who is so far God, except as Son of God, born of God, that very many heretics—as we have said—have so accepted Him as God, as to think that He must be pronounced not the Son, but the Father" (23).

He noted the following points in their doctrine: emphasis on the oneness of God, using passages such as Deuteronomy 6:4 and Galatians 3:20; emphasis on the absolute deity of Jesus as the Father incarnate, using passages such as John 10:30 and John 14:9; and identifying the title of "Son" with the Incarnation and the humanity of Christ, using Luke 1:35.

"The material of that heretical error has arisen, as I judge, from this, that they think that there is no distinction between the Son of God and the Son of man. . . . For they will have it that the self-same that is man, the Son of man, appears also as the Son of God; that man and flesh and that same frail substance may be said to be also the Son of God Himself" (24).

"For thus say they, If it is asserted that God is one, and Christ is God, then say they, If the Father and Christ be one God, Christ will be called the Father. . . . They are not willing that He should be the second person after the Father, but the Father Himself" (26). "And thus they who say that Jesus Christ is the Father argue as follows:—If God is one, and Christ is God, Christ is the Father, since God is one. If Christ be not the Father, because Christ is God the Son, there appear to be two Gods introduced, contrary to the Scriptures" (30).

Conclusions

Our investigation reveals that modalism was the dominant view among average Christians during much of the Old Catholic Age. Excluding passages in anonymous or pseudonymous literature and references to baptism in the name of Jesus, the following is a brief summary of the evidence. Significantly, this evidence does not come from advocates or promoters of modalism, who could be inclined to exaggerate, but from the most vehement opponents of modalism, who would naturally tend to minimize it as much as possible.

• Tertullian: "the majority of believers"; the doctrine was "everywhere."

• Hippolytus: "no one is ignorant" of the doctrine; it "prevail[ed]" for a time.

• Novatian: "many heretics"; "very many heretics."

• Origen: "the general run of Christian"; "many who are sincerely concerned about religion"; "scholars"; "the great multitude of those who are counted believers"; "some individuals."

• Athanasius: "so successful"; the trinitarian doctrine of the Son "was scarcely any longer preached in the churches."

The following list identifies the major beliefs that the modalists seem to have shared, followed by the names of those modalists we have specifically identified as affirming each point.

1. The absolute oneness of God (a denial of plural persons in the Godhead): Praxeas, Noetus, Zephyrinus, Callistus, Sabellius.

2. The absolute deity of Jesus (Jesus as the Father incarnate): Praxeas, Noetus, Zephyrinus, Callistus, Sabellius.

3. "Father" and "Son" refer to the same being, not two persons: Praxeas, Noetus, Callistus, Sabellius.

4. "Son" refers to the humanity of Christ, to the

Incarnation: Praxeas, Noetus, Callistus, Sabellius.

5. The Word (Logos) is not a distinct person but is the Father Himself, particularly referring to His mind, expression, action, self-revelation: Praxeas, Noetus, Callistus, Sabellius.

6. Jesus is the name by which God is revealed to us (implying baptism in Jesus' name): Praxeas, Sabellius.

7. Denial of the charge that the Father died as to His deity: Praxeas, Zephyrinus, Callistus, Sabellius.

8. The Father is the Holy Spirit: Praxeas, Callistus, Sabellius.

9. The Father is invisible, the Son is visible: Praxeas, Callistus.

From this comparison, it appears that the major modalist teachers were in agreement on the essential points of their doctrine. By contrast, the trinitarians of the age denied these points. It is also interesting to compare these positions with the teachings of Irenaeus. He definitely taught points 6 and 9. Unlike the other two major writers of this age—Tertullian and Origen—he never wrote against modalism. In reference to points 1, 2, and 5, he affirmed that God is one, that Jesus is God, and that the Word is the mind and revelation of God the Father.

It is evident that the modalists affirmed the essential tenets of Oneness, for anyone who agrees with points 1 and 2 meets the definition of Oneness given in chapter 1, and the other points follow from the first two. Moreover, Oneness adherents today affirm the nine points listed.

Some cautionary notes are in order, however. First, the historical evidence is insufficient to establish with certainty that all the modalists baptized in the name of Jesus. It appears that their doctrine requires it, that many people did so during this age, and that at least Praxeas and Sabellius did so. Second, we have no record of whether the modalists were baptized with the Holy Spirit, although a few clues in other references indicate that at least some of them were, including possibly Sabellius.[8] Third, modern Oneness does not accept the expansion-contraction, successive-manifestation theory attributed to Sabellius.

Finally, since we do not know with certainty everything the various modalists believed, it is not productive to identify modern Oneness directly with ancient modalism, Patripassianism, or Sabellianism. While the basic view of God seems to be fundamentally the same, there is no historical link. It is not appropriate to impute to the modern Oneness movement everything that the modalists taught or everything that various historians, ancient and modern, have attributed to the modalists. Oneness Pentecostals today should be evaluated by their own clearly expressed and well-documented position, not by ancient labels that mean different things to different people and that often prejudice people's thinking.

In conclusion, despite the sparseness of existing historical records, it is clear that in the Old Catholic Age many people affirmed the two central tenets of Oneness as given in chapter 1. Although some form of trinitarianism became dominant toward the end of this age, Oneness views were prevalent throughout the age and were predominant for much of the time.

Conclusion

11

The Path from Oneness to Trinity

The New Testament church was founded upon the Old Testament message of the absolute oneness of God coupled with the New Testament revelation of Jesus Christ as the fullness of the one God incarnate. The New Testament was completed and the last of the apostles died shortly before the end of the first century. Two centuries later, by the beginning of the fourth century, the predominant doctrine of God in Christendom had evolved from biblical Oneness to an incipient form of trinitarianism. This book has attempted to investigate what happened in the intervening time. In this chapter we will summarize and draw conclusions from our investigation, tracing the shift from Oneness to trinity from approximately A.D. 100 to 300.

The Post-Apostolic Age

The writers of the Post-Apostolic Age (c. A.D. 90-140) adhered closely to biblical language, usage, and thought. They affirmed the characteristic Oneness themes of strict monotheism, the absolute deity of Jesus Christ, and the true humanity of Christ. They attached great significance to the name of God and alluded to baptism in the name of

Jesus. They did not describe God as a trinity or as three persons, nor did they use any other distinctively trinitarian language. Some of their statements are incompatible with trinitarianism, and many sound like distinctive Oneness expressions today.

In short, as trinitarian scholars acknowledge, these writings express no clear concept of a trinity. Evangelical author Calvin Beisner admitted, "In the earliest times of the Church there is little explicit or precise statement, and even less definition of the doctrine of the Trinity. . . . [In the first two centuries] the primary thought was of monotheism."[1] Reformed theologian Louis Berkhof noted, "While [the Post-Apostolic Fathers] use the scriptural designation of God as Father, Son, and Holy Spirit, and also speak of Christ as God and man, they do not testify to an awareness of the implications and problems involved."[2] Similarly, Lutheran professor Otto Heick stated, "The Post-Apostolic Fathers adhered tenaciously to monotheism in the Old Testament sense. . . . These thoughts [about God] are mainly of Old Testament and Jewish origin, and exhibit little Hellenistic influence."[3]

The writings of bishops Clement of Rome, Ignatius, Polycarp, and Papias, as well as *II Clement* and the *Preaching of Peter*, are compatible with the Oneness doctrine, but statements in Ignatius, *II Clement*, and Hermas are clearly incompatible with trinitarianism. The *Didache* contains a reference to trinitarian baptism, which is probably a later insertion; if not, it indicates a gradual shift away from the original Jesus Name formula at the end of this age. Hermas and Pseudo-Barnabas may have adhered to an vague, undefined form of binitarianism, although we have shown how their statements can be interpreted in a manner consistent with Oneness. In any case, the rest of the writers, including the church leaders of the time, were simply Christocentric monotheists who did not think in trinitarian terms. Their doctrine of God was much more biblical and much less philosophical than trinitarianism is, and it corresponds most closely to the doctrine known today as Oneness.

The Age of the Greek Apologists

In the Age of the Greek Apologists (c. A.D. 130-180), we find a progressive shift away from the biblical doctrine of Oneness and the substantially identical views of the Post-Apostolic Age. The chief innovation was the doctrine of the Word (Logos) as a second divine person subordinate to the Father.

Around 130 to 150, Aristides and the *Epistle to Diognetus* still retained a predominantly biblical Oneness view, although the latter began to distinguish God from the Word. By 150 Justin and Tatian taught that the Father and the Word were two distinct persons. By 170 to 180 Theophilus and Athenagoras had begun to associate a vague, undefined form of threeness with God. Even at this date, Bishop Melito still maintained a predominantly modalist view of God.

In this age, we find the first definite modification of the baptismal formula and the first roots of the trinity. The Apologists compromised the two cardinal tenets of the biblical doctrine of Oneness: (1) They replaced God's absolute oneness with a plurality—at first two persons, beings, or gods, and later a triad of sorts. (2) They denied the absolute deity of Jesus Christ, making Him a subordinate deity. Thus we could call them subordinationistic binitarians or, later, subordinationistic triadists.

In sum, the Greek Apologists, particularly Justin, introduced several key concepts that led to trinitarianism: the Logos as a second divine person or god, the begetting of the Logos at a point in time before creation, the Logos as identical to the Son, a threefold baptismal formula, and a vague linking of the Spirit with the Father and the Son. One century after the completion of the New Testament, the stage was set for trinitarianism to emerge.

The New Catholic Encyclopedia provides an accurate summarization of the doctrine of the second century with respect to trinitarianism:

> Among the Apostolic Fathers, there had been nothing even remotely approaching such a mentality or perspective; among the second century Apologists, little more than a focusing of the problem as that of plurality within the Godhead. . . . In the last analysis, the second century theological achievement was limited. . . . A trinitarian solution was still in the future.[4]

The Old Catholic Age

In the Old Catholic Age (c. A.D. 170-325), Christendom shifted from the biblical belief in one God toward a form of trinitarianism. This process had already begun with the vague binitarian and triadic formulations of the Greek Apologists in the mid to latter part of the second century, and it culminated in the promulgation of orthodox trinitarianism in the latter part of the fourth century.

The evidence indicates that modalism was the dominant view of Christianity in the first part of this age. Since history is written by the victors, the existing evidence probably reveals only a fraction of the total scope. Nevertheless, it demonstrates that modalism was widespread throughout this period. Despite the sparseness of existing historical evidence, it is clear that in the Old Catholic Age many people affirmed the two central tenets of Oneness given in chapter 1 and many people baptized in the name of Jesus.

When trinitarianism did come, in the first part of the third century, it started with the premise that Jesus was a subordinate deity. Its two chief founders, Tertullian and Origen, never abandoned that belief. Only much later, in the fourth century, did trinitarians try to rectify this flaw, with only partial success, by affirming the coequality, coeternity, and consubstantiality of Father, Son, and Holy Spirit. Not only the Greek Apologists but also the early trinitarians rejected the unqualified statement of the Bible and the writers of the Post-Apostolic Age that Jesus is God.

At the beginning of the Old Catholic Age, Irenaeus emphasized the threefold revelation of God; however, he did not speak of a trinity of essence. He retained many important elements of earlier Oneness beliefs, particularly the following: God is one, Jesus is God, the Word is the mind and expression of the Father, the Son is the visible revelation of the invisible Father, and the name of Jesus belongs to and reveals the Father.

Irenaeus did not fully adopt the thinking of the Greek Apologists, but he was influenced by them, particularly in equating the Logos and the Son and in distinguishing the Logos from the Father in some way. Apparently, he held that the Logos was originally inherent in God and somehow became distinct for the purpose of God's self-revelation. He also apparently used a threefold baptismal formula, at least in his later years, but there is little to indicate that he thought of the Holy Spirit as a distinct person. His most significant innovation—the identification of Wisdom as the Holy Spirit—was not accepted by later trinitarians. Thus Irenaeus stands as a transitional figure between original Oneness and later trinitarianism but in a different way from the Apologists. In some ways he was still closer to Oneness; if he lived today, he might be classified within the Oneness movement as long as he baptized in the name of Jesus. He could be called at most an economic trinitarian.

More than any other theologian, Tertullian developed the terms and concepts of the trinity, yet ironically he did so as a member of a schismatic group, all the while vigorously denouncing the mainstream church. He introduced the terms "trinity, three persons, one substance" to the discussion of God. Excluding a reference in the *Didache* that is probably a corruption, he was the first to cite Matthew 28:19 as the proper baptismal formula and the first to mention triple baptism. Nevertheless, Tertullian taught that the trinity was only temporary: it had a beginning and will have an ending. Moreover, he clearly subordinated the Son and Spirit to the Father. Thus, with respect to the orthodox trinitarian doctrines of consubstantiality, coeternity, and coequality, he taught only the first, and even on that point he was aberrant since he taught that the angels participated in the one divine substance.

Origen, who was excommunicated and condemned as a heretic, made an extremely significant contribution to trinitarianism by his doctrines of the eternal Son and the eternal generation of the Son. He and Tertullian were the two most important initial advocates of trinitarianism. Like Tertullian, Origen definitely subordinated the Son and the Spirit. In terms of trinitarian orthodoxy, he taught coeternity but not coequality. While some statements seem to teach consubstantiality, others deny it.

Berkhof explained how the confusing, evolving doctrines of the Greek Apologists gradually led to the doctrine of the trinity, primarily through the later innovations of Tertullian and Origen, and how the modalistic monarchians rose up against this new doctrine:

> It may be said that [Tertullian] enlarged the doctrine of the Logos into a doctrine of the Trinity. . . .
>
> The early Church Fathers . . . had no clear conception of the Trinity. Some of them conceived of the Logos as impersonal reason, become personal at the time of creation, while others regarded Him as personal and co-eternal with the Father, sharing the divine essence, and yet ascribed to Him a certain subordination to the Father. The Holy Spirit occupied no important place in their discussions at all. . . . Tertullian was the first to assert clearly the tri-personality of God, and to maintain the substantial unity of the three Persons. But even he did not reach a clear statement of the doctrine of the Trinity.
>
> Meanwhile Monarchianism came along with its emphasis on the unity of God and on the true deity of Christ, involving a denial of the Trinity in the proper sense of the word. Tertullian and Hippolytus combatted their views in the West, while Origen struck

them a decisive blow in the East. . . . But even Origen's construction of the doctrine of the Trinity was not altogether satisfactory. . . . While he was the first to explain the relation of the Father to the Son by employing the idea of eternal generation, he defined this so as to involve the subordination of the Second Person to the First in respect to essence.[5]

Except for Commodian, the later writers of the Old Catholic Age spoke more and more in trinitarian terms. They typically subordinated the Son and Spirit to the Father and did not have a clear doctrine of the Holy Spirit. Novatian, another schismatic, contributed significantly to the development of trinitarianism by emphasizing the distinction of persons and by emphasizing the Holy Spirit as a third person, but he still retained subordinationism.

Of all the writers of this age, only Dionysius of Rome and possibly Gregory Thaumaturgus seemed to define trinitarianism in a way compatible with later orthodoxy. In particular, the controversy between Dionysius of Rome and Dionysius of Alexandria prepared the way for the decision at the Council of Nicea.

In short, the Old Catholic Age produced the first definite trinitarians, who clashed first with the monarchians, especially the modalists, and then with the Arians. By the end of the age, some form of trinitarianism and trinitarian baptism had become dominant in Christendom, but it took most of the fourth century to formulate and establish orthodox trinitarianism.

In contrast to the biblical doctrine of Oneness, the trinitarians of the Old Catholic Age (1) divided the personality of God and (2) denied the full deity of Jesus Christ.

Relative to the first point, they often used tritheistic language such as the following: the Father and the Son are "two separate persons" and "two different beings" (Tertullian); the Son is "one individual produced from a different one" (Hippolytus); the Word is a "second God," "a separate entity," and "a separate being [who] has an essence of His own" (Origen).

Relative to the second point, the early trinitarians spoke of the deity of Jesus as "created" (Tertullian and Origen); not as old, strong, noble, powerful, or great as the Father, "a derivation," "a portion of the whole Godhead," and not "God Himself, the Lord Almighty" (Tertullian); "born" (Tertullian, Origen, and Novatian); "inferior" (Origen and Novatian); not eternal (Tertullian, Hippolytus, and Novatian); subject to the Father (Origen and Hippolytus); "made God," a "second God," "a god," not "the most High God," and God only in a relative sense (Origen). Although the later doctrines of consubstantiality, coequality, and coeternity mitigated this error somewhat, it is clear that trinitarianism was originally formulated by people who did not accept the absolute deity of Jesus Christ.

To the Council of Nicea and Beyond

Toward the end of the Old Catholic Age, a fierce controversy over the doctrine of God erupted between two men of Alexandria: Athanasius, an archdeacon, who was supported by Bishop Alexander, and Arius, a presbyter. Arius taught that Christ is an intermediate divine being created by the Father, who is subordinate to the Father and who is of a similar, but not the same, essence. Like the dynamic monarchians he tried to uphold God's oneness by denying the true deity of Christ, and like the trinitarians he held that Christ is a second person. In opposition to Arius, Athanasius affirmed that the Father and the Son are two distinct persons who are coequal, coeternal, and of the same substance.

The view of Athanasius prevailed at the first ecumenical council, held in Nicea in 325, making him the father of trinitarian orthodoxy. The issue was not finally resolved, however, until the Council of Constantinople in 381, which affirmed the decision of Nicea and clarified the identity of the Holy Spirit as the third coequal person of the trinity. The result was the revised Nicene Creed used today.

The most definitive trinitarian creed—used by both Roman Catholics and Protestants, including evangelicals—is the so-called Athanasian creed. It can be no earlier than the fifth century, and it appeared in final form in the late eighth or early ninth century. These two creeds define orthodox trinitarianism today.

The How and the Why

Let us summarize briefly the major steps in the development of trinitarianism.

1. About 150 the Greek Apologists, particularly Justin, defined the Word to be the Son, described the Word/Son as a second divine being begotten by God the Father at a point in time before creation, and said that the Word was subordinate to God. A threefold baptismal formula was introduced, along with some vague notions of threeness in relation to God.

2. About 210 Tertullian introduced the term *trinity* and formulated the concept of one God in three persons.

In his trinity, the Father alone is eternal, and He is superior to the other two persons.

3. About 230 Origen likewise promoted trinitarianism, contributing the key doctrines of the eternal Son and the eternal generation of the Son. He thereby prepared the way for elevating the status of the second person, although he himself still taught that the Father was superior to the other two persons.

4. Under the influence of Athanasius, the Council of Nicea in 325 rejected Arianism. It declared that the Father and the Son were of the same substance, making them equal. (Dionysius of Rome had earlier expressed much the same concept in an effort to refute both modalism and tritheism.)

5. The Council of Constantinople in 381 followed the doctrine of Athanasius and the Cappadocians (Gregory of Nyssa, Gregory Nazianzus, and Basil of Caesarea). It clarified the status of the Holy Spirit and placed all three persons on an equal footing.

6. Produced sometime in the fifth to eighth centuries, the Athanasian Creed put in definitive form the doctrine of the victors of Nicea and Constantinople, declaring the coequality, coeternity, and consubstantiality of the three persons.

Why did this doctrine develop as it did? The impetus for the first of the foregoing steps was the Greek philosophical concept of the Logos. Under its influence, the scriptural distinction between God and His Son, which related to the Incarnation, was wrongly imputed to the divine nature of God Himself. In seeking to analyze the New Testament by pagan categories of thought instead of by the context of Scripture itself, including the prior revelation of the Old Testament, and by the illumination of the Holy Spirit, the forerunners of trinitarianism failed to understand the Incarnation.

Why did these early theologians make such a blunder? They failed to purge themselves of the pagan ideas of their own past and culture. Instead of relying on the transforming power of the Holy Spirit, they tried too hard to be intellectually pleasing to their culture and society. Psychologically, it seems that they prided themselves on their great human learning and reasoning and so were led astray by these very things. For example, Justin made clear to everyone that he was a philosopher, and Tertullian and Origen were openly contemptuous of the majority of believers and derided their ignorance.

Why did Christian believers accept this elitist doctrine? The answer is that for about a century they did not. When they finally did, it seems that the compromise had much to do with a general spiritual decline. As time went on it appears that people relied less and less upon the power of the Holy Spirit, and the great outpouring of the Spirit subsided. By the time trinitarianism finally became dominant, in the fourth century, it seems that the baptism of the Holy Spirit with the initial sign of speaking in tongues was an experience of the past as far as most people were concerned. Masses of pagans joined the institutional church with little or no repentance or regeneration by the Spirit, and the church as a whole became susceptible to pagan influences and modes of thought. The prevailing polytheism of the culture made trinitarianism seem quite plausible, especially when converts had little or no personal relationship with the one God.

Once the concept of plurality was introduced to the

discussion of the Godhead, it was easy for the initial binitarian emphasis eventually to become trinitarian. Scriptural statements relative to the Word/Son were interpreted in a new way, and when this new mode of thinking was applied to scriptural statements about the Holy Spirit, similar results followed. According to the new doctrine, the Father was the supreme God, as distinguished from Jesus. One way adherents expressed their thinking was to modify the practice of baptizing in the name of Jesus only, for this formula indicated that Jesus alone was the Savior and the sole object of faith for remission of sins. The only alternative they could find with a scriptural basis was the words of Matthew 28:19, which led them to adopt a threefold baptismal formula (rather than merely a twofold formula). Thus a threefold formula preceded a conscious confession of trinitarianism. Again, once the threefold formula was used to teach a personal distinction between the Father and the Son, it followed that the Holy Spirit was personally distinct as well.

The very basis upon which the concept of a plurality in God was introduced—the Apologists' Logos doctrine—logically required that the second person be viewed as subordinate, created, inferior, and a derivation from the first person. Thus it was natural for subordinationism to remain an integral part of trinitarianism for about a century.

However, this aspect of trinitarianism clashed violently with many scriptural statements of the absolute deity of Jesus Christ and with the historic practical piety of the common believers, who prayed to Jesus as God and Savior. As a result, trinitarianism was quite vulnerable to attack by the modalists. On the other hand, people such as the Arians took the subordinationistic element of trinitarianism to its logical extreme, totally denying the deity of Jesus.

In an effort to protect the deity of Jesus Christ as much as possible given their uncompromising commitment to the concept of plural persons in the Godhead, the trinitarians eventually formulated the concepts of co-equality, coeternity, and consubstantiality. If Jesus was indeed a second person and if He was indeed God in some sense, then He had to be equal in every way to the first person. In the case of the Holy Spirit, the popular pressure was not as strong, but the same reasoning was eventually applied.

In sum, trinitarianism developed logically from a flawed premise of plural persons in the Godhead. It has reached an equilibrium state in that once a person accepts the proposition that one God can and does exists as three persons, then the other definitions and conclusions follow. But when someone stands outside the system and views it as a whole, it is evident that trinitarianism is contrary to Scripture, that its axioms are inherently self-contradictory and incomprehensible, and that its definitions and propositions have no objective meaning.

For example, in the final analysis the only distinction between the three persons is that the Father is unbegotten, the Son is begotten, and the Holy Spirit is proceeding. But what does it mean to say that the Son is begotten, that the Son is eternally being begotten, and that the Holy Spirit is proceeding? What is the difference between being begotten and proceeding? How do these terms avoid some sort of subordination of the Son and Spirit to the Father? What passages of Scripture explain the meaning of these terms or concepts? If we cannot attach any objective, comprehensible meaning to these concepts, then how can we identify the distinctions within God's being that these terms supposedly prove?

In short, the root problem of the trinitarian error, both historically and theologically, is a failure to heed and comprehend Colossians 2:8-10: "Beware lest any man spoil you through philosophy and vain deceit, after the tradition of men, after the rudiments of the world, and not after Christ. For in him dwelleth all the fulness of the Godhead bodily. And ye are complete in him, which is the head of all principality and power."

Postscript

Although by the end of the fourth century trinitarianism was solidly established and triumphant, the existence of the Bible and the illumination of the Holy Spirit ensured that the Oneness message would not die completely. Throughout subsequent centuries, Oneness concepts and baptism in the name of Jesus continued to surface.[6] In the twentieth century, the great outpouring of the Holy Spirit has ushered in a renewed understanding of the biblical message of the absolute oneness of God and the absolute deity of the Lord Jesus Christ.

Notes

Chapter 1. Studying Oneness and Trinity in Ancient Writings

[1]"Trinity, Holy," *The New Catholic Encyclopedia* (New York: McGraw Hill, 1967), 14:295.

[2]Van Harvey, *A Handbook of Theological Terms* (New York: Macmillan, 1964), 244.

[3]Ibid.; William Stevens, *Doctrines of the Christian Religion* (Nashville: Broadman, 1967), 119.

[4]Louis Berkhof, *Systematic Theology* (Grand Rapids: Eerdmans, 1941), 87.

[5]Charles Hodge, *Systematic Theology* (Reprint, Grand Rapids: Eerdmans, 1986), 1:444; Augustus Strong, *Systematic Theology* (Old Tappan, N.J.: Revell, 1907), 304; Harvey, 245.

[6]Otto Heick, *A History of Christian Thought* (Philadelphia: Fortress Press, 1965), 1:160; "Trinity," *Encyclopedia of Religion and Ethics*, ed. James Hastings et al. (New York: Charles Scribner's Sons, 1951), 11:459-60; Hodge, 1:445; Berkhof, *Systematic Theology*, 89.

[7]"Trinity," *Encyclopedia of Religion and Ethics*, 11:460.

[8]E. H. Klotsche, *The History of Christian Doctrine*, rev. ed. (Grand Rapids: Baker, 1979), 17-18; Heick, 1:44-46.

[9]Klotsche, 23-24; Heick, 1:58-59.

[10]Heick, 1:64-65.

[11]Klotsche, 27.

[12]Louis Berkhof, *The History of Christian Doctrines* (Grand Rapids: Baker, 1937), 59-60.

[13]Heick, 1:106.

[14]Gregory Boyd, "The Pseudo-Apostolic Faith of the United Pentecostal Church and the Witness of Second-Century Christianity" (Paper presented at the second ARC [Apologetic Research Coalition] Symposium on Cults, the Occult and World Religions, Farmington Hills, Mich., 10 August 1989), 2-3. Emphasis is original.

Chapter 2. Clement, Ignatius, Polycarp, and Hermas

[1]Unless otherwise indicated, all quotations of ante-Nicene writings are from Alexander Roberts, James Donaldson, and A. Cleveland Coxe, eds., *The Ante-Nicene Fathers* (1885; reprint, Grand Rapids: Eerdmans, 1981). Parenthetical numbers after quotes refer to chapters; numbers separated by a colon refer to chapter and verse; book and chapter; or book, chapter, and verse. Parentheses inside quotes represent parentheses or brackets used by the original editors.

[2]Cyril Richardson et al., trans. and ed., *Early Christian Fathers* (New York: Macmillan, 1970), 73.

[3]*Ante-Nicene Fathers*, 1:31, 45.

[4]Richardson, 81, 83.

[5]J. B. Lightfoot and J. R. Harmer, eds., *The Apostolic Fathers* (1891; reprint, Grand Rapids: Baker, 1988), 144.

[6]Joseph Thayer, *A Greek-English Lexicon of the New Testament* (1889; reprint, Grand Rapids: Zondervan, n.d.), 477. Emphasis added.

[7]*The Lost Books of the Bible and the Forgotten Books of Eden* (New York: William Collins, 1963), 173. Information supplied by William Chalfant.

[8]Richardson, 143.

Chapter 3. Anonymous and Pseudonymous Writings

[1]E. Calvin Beisner, *God in Three Persons* (Wheaton, Ill.: Tyndale, 1984), 47.

[2]Jim Beverley, "Truly Pentecostal? A Critique of the United Pentecostal Church," *The Journal of Pastoral Practice*, 4, no. 3 (1980): 109.

[3]Richardson, 161.

[4]M. B. Riddle, in *Ante-Nicene Fathers*, 7:375.

[5]Ibid.

[6]Richardson, 165.

[7]Riddle, in *Ante-Nicene Fathers*, 7:374.

[8]Kirsopp Lake, "Baptism (Early Christian)," *Encyclopedia of Religion and Ethics*, 2:389.

[9]J. V. Bartlet, "Baptism (New Testament)," *Encyclopedia of Religion and Ethics*, 2:378.

[10]Klotsche, 17.

[11]Heick, 1:53, 87.

Chapter 4. Justin

[1]For documentation of this paragraph, see Philip Schaff, *History of the Christian Church* (Grand Rapids: Eerdmans, 1910), 2:714-15.

[2]For a description of the views of Plato and Philo, see Klotsche, 8, 13; Heick, 1:25, 31.

[3]Richardson, 233.

[4]Ibid., 245.

Chapter 5. Other Writings of the Age

[1]Berkhof, *History of Christian Doctrines*, 58.

[2]Heick, 1:60-61.

[3]Ibid., 1:61.

Chapter 6. Irenaeus

[1]Heick, 1:109-10.

[2]Richardson, 347.

³Ibid.

⁴*See* Berkhof, *History of Christian Doctrines*, 64-65; Heick, 1:108.

⁵*Ante-Nicene Fathers*, 1:311-12.

⁶Theophilus possibly referred to the Holy Spirit as Wisdom in *To Autolycus*, 2:15 and 2:18, but the reference is uncertain, as shown by 2:10 and 2:22.

⁷Heick, 1:109, 127.

⁸Joseph P. Smith, trans., Irenaeus, *Demonstration of the Apostolic Preaching*, (Westminster, Md.: Newman Press, 1952), 7-8.

⁹Heick, 1:108.

¹⁰Schaff, *History*, 2:569.

Chapter 7. Early Trinitarians: Tertullian, Origen, and Others

¹Klotsche, 52-53; Heick, 1: 123, 127; Schaff, *History*, 2:819.

²Heick, 1:127.

³Jaroslav Pelikan, *The Emergence of the Catholic Tradition (100-600)*, vol. 1 of *The Christian Tradition: A History of the Development of Doctrine* (Chicago: University of Chicago Press, 1971), 105.

⁴Ibid., 101.

⁵Heick, 1:114.

⁶Pelikan, 191.

⁷Schaff, *History*, 2:552.

⁸Pelikan, 192.

⁹Schaff, *History*, 2:797-99.

¹⁰Berkhof, *History of Christian Doctrines*, 65, 83.

¹¹Ibid., 83-84.

Chapter 8. Baptism in the Name of Jesus.

¹Walter Bauer, W. F. Arndt, F. W. Gingrich, and F. W. Danker,

A Greek-English Lexicon of the New Testament and Other Early Christian Literature, 2nd ed. (Chicago: University of Chicago Press, 1979), 571-73; Heick, 1:53, 87; J. F. Bethune-Baker, *An Introduction to the Early History of Christian Doctrine* (London: Methuen and Company, 1933), 25, 378; Kirsopp Lake, in *Encyclopedia of Religion and Ethics,* 2:389; Jean Danielou, *The Theology of Jewish Christianity,* vol. 1 of *The Development of Christian Doctrine Before the Council of Nicaea,* John A. Baker, ed. and trans. (London: Darton, Lonman, and Todd, 1964), 323; Wilhelm Bousset, *Kyrios Christianity—A History of the Belief in Christ from, the Beginning of Christianity to Irenaeus,* 5th ed., trans. John Steely (New York: Abingdon, 1970), 292; David A. Reed, *Origins and Development of the Theology of Oneness Pentecostalism in the United States* (Ann Arbor, Mich.: University Microfilms International, 1978), 220; Williston Walker, *A History of the Christian Church* (New York: Charles Scribner's Sons, 1947), 58. For further citations, see William Chalfant, *Ancient Champions of Oneness* (1979; reprint, Hazelwood, Mo.: Word Aflame Press, 1982), chap. 5.

[2]James M. Robinson, ed., *The Nag Hammadi Library in English* (New York: Harper and Row, 1978), 147.

Chapter 9. Oneness Concepts in Popular Belief

[1]*See* Pelikan, 178-79.

[2]Gregory Boyd, "The Oneness View of the Ante-Nicene Fathers: A Critical Appraisal," in "Papers presented to the First Occasional Symposium on Aspects of the Oneness Pentecostal Movement" [held at Harvard Divinity School, July 5-7, 1984] (Cambridge, Mass.: Jeffrey Gill, 1984), 183-84.

[3]Johannes Quasten, *Patrology* (Westminster, Md.: Newman Press, 1963), 3:98-99.

[4]Philip Schaff and Henry Wace, eds., *The Nicene and Post-Nicene Fathers,* 2d. ser. (Reprint, Grand Rapids: Eerdmans,

1976), 14:185. Unless otherwise indicated, all quotations of Nicene and post-Nicene writings are from this work. Parenthetical numbers after quotes refer to book and chapter, or book, chapter, and paragraph. Parentheses inside quotes represent parentheses or brackets used by the editors.

[5]Pelikan, 104.

[6]Ibid., 104-5.

[7]"Monarchianism," *Encyclopoedia Britannica* (Chicago: William Benton, 1964), 15:686.

[8]"Monarchianism," *The New Schaff-Herzog Encyclopedia of Religious Knowledge*, ed. Samuel Jackson (Grand Rapids: Baker, 1963), 7:454-58.

[9]Heick, 1:147, 149.

[10]Pelikan, 178-79.

[11]Adolph Harnack, *History of Dogma* (London: Williams and Norgate, 1897), 3:51-54.

[12]Heick, 1:149.

[13]Schaff, *History*, 2:572-73.

[14]Berkhof, *History of Christian Doctrines*, 78.

[15]Chalfant, 105-13.

[16]Jules Lebreton and Jacques Zeiller, A *History of the Early Church* (New York: Collier, 1962), 4:148.

[17]Schaff, *History*, 2:856.

[18]H. A. Wolfson, *The Philosophy of the Church Fathers* (Cambridge, Mass.: Harvard University Press, 1970), 1:583-84.

Chapter 10. Teachers of Modalism: Praxeas, Noetus, and Sabellius

[1]Lebreton and Zeiller, 4:149.

[2]*Nicene and Post-Nicene Fathers*, 2d. ser., 7:350.

[3]Pelikan, 179.

[4]Heick, 1:150-51.

[5]Berkhof, 79.

[6]J. A. Dorner, *Doctrine of the Person of Christ* (Edinburgh: T. and T. Clark, 1870), 2:164.

[7]"Monarchianism," *Encyclopedia of Religion and Ethics*, ed. James Hastings (New York: Charles Scribner's Sons, 1962), 8:780.

[8]At least some of the Montanists were modalists, and they emphasized the Holy Spirit with tongues. (See chapter 9.) Although Tertullian stated that Praxeas opposed the Montanists, he did not rebuke the modalists for lack of spiritual gifts (including tongues), as he did the Marcionites in his tract against them *(Against Marcion* 5:8). Epiphanius said that Sabellius taught regeneration by the Holy Spirit. (See Chalfant, 133, 135.) Pseudo-Athanasius recorded a reference of Sabellius to the spiritual gifts of I Corinthians 12 *(Orations against the Arians* 4:25).

Chapter 11. The Path from Oneness to Trinity

[1]Beisner, 47-48.

[2]Berkhof, *History of Christian Doctrines*, 40.

[3]Heick, 1:46-47.

[4]"Trinity, Holy," *New Catholic Encyclopedia*, 14:295-305.

[5]Berkhof, *History of Christian Doctrines*, 65, 83-84.

[6]*See* David Bernard, *The Oneness of God* (Hazelwood, Mo.: Word Aflame Press, 1983), 241-52; David Bernard, *The New Birth* (Hazelwood, Mo.: Word Aflame Press, 1984), 271-77.

Select Bibliography

Primary Sources

Irenaeus. *Demonstration of the Apostolic Preaching.* Translated by Joseph P. Smith. Westminster, Md.: Newman Press, 1952.

Lightfoot, J. B., and J. R. Harmer, eds. *The Apostolic Fathers.* 1891. Reprint. Grand Rapids: Baker, 1988. [Greek and English]

Richardson, Cyril, et al., trans. and eds. *Early Christian Fathers.* New York: Macmillan, 1970.

Roberts, Alexander, James Donaldson, and A. Cleveland Coxe, eds. *The Ante-Nicene Fathers.* 1885. Reprint. Grand Rapids: Eerdmans, 1981.

Robinson, James M., ed. *The Nag Hammadi Library in English.* New York: Harper and Row, 1978.

Schaff, Philip, and Henry Wace, eds. *The Nicene and Post-Nicene Fathers.* 2d ser. Reprint. Grand Rapids: Eerdmans, 1976.

Secondary Sources

Bauer, Walter, W. F. Arndt, F. W. Gingrich, and F. W. Danker. *A Greek-English Lexicon of the New Testament and Other Early Christian Literature.* 2d ed. Chicago: University of Chicago Press, 1979.

Berkhof, Louis. *The History of Christian Doctrines.* Grand Rapids: Baker, 1937

– – – – . *Systematic Theology.* Grand Rapids: Eerdmans, 1941.

Beisner, Calvin. *God in Three Persons.* Wheaton, Ill.: Tyndale, 1984.

Bernard, David. *The New Birth.* Hazelwood, Mo.: Word Aflame Press, 1984.

– – – – .*The Oneness of God.* Hazelwood, Mo.: Word Aflame Press, 1983.

Bethune-Baker, J. F. *An Introduction to the Early History of Christian Doctrine.* London: Methuen and Company, 1933.

Chalfant, William. *Ancient Champions of Oneness.* 1979. Reprint. Hazelwood, Mo.: Word Aflame Press, 1982.

Dorner, J. A. *Doctrine of the Person of Christ.* Edinburgh: T. and T. Clark, 1870.

Harnack, Adolph. *History of Dogma.* London: Williams and Norgate, 1897.

Harvey, Van. *A Handbook of Theological Terms.* New York: Macmillan, 1964.

Hastings, James, et al., eds. *Encyclopedia of Religion and Ethics.* New York: Charles Scribner's Sons, 1951.

Heick, Otto. *A History of Christian Thought.* Philadelphia: Fortress Press, 1965.

Hodge, Charles, *Systematic Theology.* Reprint. Grand Rapids: Eerdmans, 1986.

Klotsche, E. H. *The History of Christian Doctrine.* Rev. ed. Grand Rapids: Baker, 1979.

Lebreton, Jules, and Jacques Zeiller. *A History of the Early Church.* New York: Collier, 1962.

Pelikan, Jaroslav. *The Emergence of the Catholic Tradition (100-600).* Vol. 1 of *The Christian Tradition: A History of the Development of Doctrine.* Chicago: University of Chicago Press, 1971.

Quasten, Johannes. *Patrology.* Westminster, Md.: Newman Press, 1963.

Schaff, Philip. *History of the Christian Church.* Grand Rapids: Eerdmans, 1910.

Stevens, William. *Doctrines of the Christian Religion.* Nashville: Broadman, 1967.

Strong, Augustus. *Systematic Theology.* Old Tappan, N.J.: Revell, 1907.

Walker, Williston. A *History of the Christian Church.* New York: Charles Scribner's Sons, 1947.

Wolfson, H. A. *The Philosophy of the Church Fathers.* Cambridge, Mass.: Harvard University Press, 1970.

Glossary

Apologist. One who defends a belief against intellectual objections. *See* Greek Apologists.

Arianism. The doctrine of Arius (280?-336), a presbyter at Alexandria. Arius held that there is only one God and that the Son or Word is a divine being like God but created by God. Thus Jesus is a demigod. This view was condemned at the Council of Nicea in 325 and again at the Council of Constantinople in 381.

Binitarianism. The belief in two persons in the Godhead, usually the Father and the Son (or Word).

Christocentric. An adjective to describe a doctrinal system in which the person and work of Christ are the foundation and focus of everything.

Coequality. The orthodox trinitarian belief that each person of the trinity is equal to the other in power and attributes.

Coeternity. The orthodox trinitarian belief that each person of the trinity has always existed and always will exist.

Constantinople, Council of. Ecumenical church council in 381 that affirmed the Council of Nicea and more clearly defined orthodox trinitarianism. It particularly established that the Holy Spirit was the third coequal person.

Consubstantiality. The orthodox trinitarian belief that in each person of the trinity the same divine substance or essence is fully contained. There are three persons but only one substance.

Ditheism. The belief in two gods.

Dynamic monarchianism. A belief in ancient history that Jesus was a human being who became the Son of God by reason of the indwelling of divine wisdom or the Logos. Apparently, the dynamic monarchians did not consider Jesus to be God in the strict sense of the word.

Economic Trinitarianism. See Trinitarianism, Economic.

Gnosticism. An ancient system of belief that combined elements from Greek philosophy, Oriental mysticism, and eventually Christianity. It taught the following: the world is composed of spirit and matter, spirit is good, matter is evil, salvation consists in deliverance of the spirit from matter, and salvation is achieved by means of a secret or higher knowledge (Greek, *gnosis)*.

Greek Apologists. Writers from approximately 130 to 180 who wrote treatises in Greek defending Christianity against attacks by pagan philosophers and writers.

Logos, Greek term meaning "word." In John 1:1, the term refers to God Himself, particularly with reference to His mind, plan, and self-revelation. In ancient Greek philosophy it meant reason as the controlling principle of the universe. The Greek Apologists equated the Logos with the Son and said the Logos was a subordinate second person in the Godhead. Trinitarianism also equates the Logos with the Son as the second person of the trinity.

Modalism, modalistic monarchianism. A belief in ancient history that Father, Son, and Holy Spirit are not distinctions in God's nature or self-conscious persons but simply *modes* (methods, manifestations) of God's activity. As a corollary, Jesus Christ is all the fullness of the Godhead, or the Father, incarnate.

Monarchianism. A belief in ancient history that emphasized the undivided oneness and sovereignty *(monarchia)* of God. It opposed the emerging doctrine of the trinity. Historians identify two sharply differing forms of monarchianism: dynamic and modalistic.

Montanism. An ancient movement in Christendom that broke away from the institutional church around 177. The Montanists emphasized the work and gifts of the Spirit, including speaking in tongues; the priesthood of all believers; the imminent return of Jesus Christ; and a life of strict morality, which later tended to legalism and asceticism.

Monotheism. The belief in only one God.

Nicea, Council of. First ecumenical church council in Christendom, held in the town of Nicea in 325. It condemned Arianism, asserting that the Father and Son are of the same substance. It is regarded as the first official endorsement of trinitarianism.

Nicene Creed. Definitive statement of orthodox trinitarianism that resulted from the Council of Nicea in 325 and the Council of Constantinople in 381.

Old Catholic Age. Era from approximately 170 to 325 in which theologians in Christendom began to develop a formal doctrinal system to define *catholic* (universal) orthodoxy against various heresies.

Oneness. The belief that God is absolutely one with no distinction of persons and that Jesus is the fullness of the Godhead incarnate.

Polytheism. The belief in more than one god.

Post-Apostolic Age. The generation after the death of the last apostle, John. The leaders and writers of this age were active from approximately 90 to 140. The most prominent writers were Clement of Rome, Ignatius, Polycarp, and Hermas.

Subordinationism. The belief that one person in the Godhead is inferior to, subject to, lesser than, or created by another person in the Godhead. This view presupposes a plurality of persons in the Godhead. The Greek Apologists and the early trinitarians subordinated the Word (second person) to the Father (first person).

Triad. A group of three. This book uses the term to describe the view of writers who vaguely associated some sort of threeness with God without defining God to be three persons.

Trinitarianism. The belief that there is one God who exists as three persons: Father, Son (or Word), and Holy Ghost (or Holy Spirit). Orthodox trinitarianism today holds that the three persons are coequal, coeternal, and consubstantial.

Trinitarianism, Economic. A form of trinitarianism that distinguishes the divine persons on the basis of God's activity or operations in the world rather than His essence.

Tritheism. The belief in three gods.

Unitarianism. The belief that God is only one person and that Jesus Christ is not God.

Word. See Logos.

Index